Student Workbook

for

Basics of Social Research
Qualitative and Quantitative Approaches

Second Edition

W. Lawrence Neuman
University of Wisconsin—Whitewater

PEARSON

Boston   New York   San Francisco
Mexico City   Montreal   Toronto   London   Madrid   Munich   Paris
Hong Kong   Singapore   Tokyo   Cape Town   Sydney

Copyright © 2007 Pearson Education, Inc.

All rights reserved. No part of the material protected by this copyright notice may be reproduced or utilized in any form or by any means, electronic or mechanical, including photocopying, recording, or by any information storage and retrieval system, without written permission from the copyright owner.

To obtain permission(s) to use material from this work, please submit a written request to Allyn and Bacon, Permissions Department, 75 Arlington Street, Boston, MA 02116 or fax your request to 617-848-7320.

ISBN-10: 0-205-52912-7
ISBN-13: 978-0-205-52912-4

Printed in the United States of America

10 9 8 7 6 5 4 3 2 1   10 09 08 07 06

FOREWORD TO THE STUDENT

For each book chapter, you will find a list of learning objectives, the key term list from the end of each chapter with definitions for matching, and activities or exercises. The following are suggestions to help you learn the material and study a chapter:

1. First, review the Chapter Outline in the textbook to get a general idea of what the chapter covers.

2. Read through the entire chapter slowly from beginning to end. Read subheadings and take notes on the key ideas, terms or principles by restating them in your own words or with your own examples. Also, write down questions to bring to your class for discussion.

3. After finishing the chapter, read the list of Key Terms at the end. If there is any that you do not know or about which you are uncertain, go back to find it in the chapter.

4. In this Workbook, first read the Learning Objectives for the chapter. Can you do each of the things listed? If not, return to the textbook chapter and reread relevant sections.

5. Complete the Matching Key Terms for each chapter. To do this, read each definition and match it to a term without looking at the chapter. If you are unsure of the answers, go back to the chapter to check your answers. Once you are confident, see how well you did by looking up the answers in the back of the workbook.

6. Complete the Exercises assigned by your teacher and any you find of interest.

7. Do the Practice Quizzes and afterward look up answers at the back of this workbook.

8. Explore the Internet links on the CD that comes with this workbook.

USING THE CD

This workbook comes with a Windows compatible CD. The CD contains the following:

1. **SPSS** (statistical software program) version for student use.
   This is designed to be installed on the hard drive of a PC and run from it. You will need to run its install program.

2. **SPSS data files**.
   There are two data files based on GSS (General Social Survey) that are described in Appendix B of this workbook.

3. **Sample program**.
   A small, simple program for drawing random numbers when doing probability sampling.

4. **Student Workbook Internet Links.**
   Files that can be read using Microsoft Explorer™. You will begin with a file that called OPEN WORKBOOK. It has a Table of Contents that allows you to jump to the various workbook chapters (Note: because of the varying size of the contents in these files, one file has a combination of three workbook chapters, two divide up chapters into two segments). Each chapter file has links to various Internet sites. Once in a chapter file, you can click on an icon at the bottom that takes you back to the Table of Contents.

   Since this part is designed for use with the Internet use it on a microcomputer that is connected to the Internet. To open it in Microsoft Windows™ go to the CD, locate the file called OPEN WORKBOOK and click quickly twice on the file name. Your computer should load its browser (Netscape Navigator™ or Microsoft Explorer™) and open the file. Exercises in the print version of the workbook refer directly to some chapters on the CD. They are listed below and marked with a CD symbol. Most other exercises in the workbook do not.

Workbook exercises that require use of the CD

Exercise 1.2
Exercises 3.2, 3.4
Exercises 5.4, 5.6
Exercise 6.1
Exercises 7.2, 7.3, 7.4, 7.5
Exercises 9.1, 9.3, 9.4, 9.5
Exercises 10.1, 10.2, 10.3
Exercise 11.3
Exercises 12.2, 12.4

CONTENTS

CHAPTER 1:
SCIENCE AND RESEARCH 1

CHAPTER 2:
THEORY AND RESEARCH 9

CHAPTER 3:
ETHICS IN SOCIAL RESEARCH 18

CHAPTER 4:
REVIEWING THE SCHOLARLY LITERATURE
AND PLANNING A STUDY 22

CHAPTER 5:
QUALITATIVE AND QUANTITATIVE MEASUREMENT 39

CHAPTER 6:
QUALITATIVE AND QUANTITATIVE SAMPLING 52

CHAPTER 7:
SURVEY RESEARCH 67

CHAPTER 8:
EXPERIMENTAL RESEARCH 74

CHAPTER 9:
NONREACTIVE RESEARCH AND SECONDARY ANALYSIS 86

CHAPTER 10:
ANALYZING QUANTITATIVE DATA 94

CHAPTER 11:
FIELD RESEARCH 110

CHAPTER 12:
HISTORICAL-COMPARATIVE RESEARCH 117

CHAPTER 13:
ANALYZING QUALITATIVE DATA 121

CHAPTER 14:
WRITING THE RESEARCH REPORT 126

APPENDIX A:
ANSWERS TO PRACTICE QUIZZES AND MATCHING 131

APPENDIX B:
CONTENTS OF DATA FILES 143

CHAPTER 1

SCIENCE AND RESEARCH

LEARNING OBJECTIVES

After studying Chapter 1 you will be able to do the following
1. Distinguish between social research and alternative ways to gain knowledge about the social world, and explain why science is usually superior;
2. Understand how the scientific method applies to the study of the social world and the role of the scientific community;
3. Identify and correctly place the steps of research in sequence;
4. Understand the meaning of "empirical data;"
5. Distinguish between quantitative and qualitative social research;
6. Describe the goals of exploratory, descriptive and explanatory research, and recognize study types;
7. Understand basic and applied research and identify at least five areas where they differ;
8. Describe types of applied research and explain how each is used;
9. Understand how cross-sectional, time series, panel and case study research differ;
10. Identify a research project as being an experiment, a survey, content analysis, existing statistics, field research, or comparative-historical research

KEY TERM MATCHING DEFINITIONS, CHAPTER 1

1. Events and things that we can observe and experience through the human senses (e.g., touch, sight, hearing, smell, taste).
2. A collection of interacting people who share a system of rules and attitudes that sustain the process of producing scientific knowledge.
3. Numerical and non-numerical information and evidence that have been carefully gathered according to established procedures.
4. The tendency to take notice of certain people or events based upon past experience or attitudes.
5. Information that is in the form of numbers.
6. Accepting broad statements about the social world based upon a narrow perspective or very few cases.
7. A tendency to accept information quickly and failing to investigate it to the degree of depth demanded by scientific standards.
8. The process of creating new knowledge using the ideas, techniques, and rules of the scientific community.
9. A tendency to allow the positive reputation of people, places or things to "rub off" or color our thinking and judgments instead of remaining completely neutral.

10. Research that involves a way of thinking and asking questions about the social world and a set of processes for creating new scientifically-based knowledge.
11. Research in which one studies a few people or cases in great detail over time.
12. A type of qualitative research in which a researcher directly observes the people being studied in a natural setting for an extended period. Often by the researcher combines intense observing with participation in their social activities.
13. A type of applied research in which one tries to determine how well a program or policy is working, or reaching its goals and objectives.
14. Longitudinal research in which the exact same cases or people are observed at multiple points in time.
15. Research that is like a "snapshot;" it looks at a single point in time.
16. Research that we use to solve a concrete problem or address a policy question and has a direct, practical application.
17. Research in which we examine different cultures or time periods to better understand the social world.
18. Research that advances knowledge of the fundamentals of how the social world works and develops general theoretical explanations.
19. Research in which we intervene or do something to one group of people but not to another, then we compare results for the two groups to see the effect of our intervention.
20. Research that focuses on why events occur or tries to test and build social theory.
21. Quantitative research in which we systematically ask many people the same questions, record responses, then analyze the answers.
22. Research in which we "paint a picture" with words or numbers, present a profile, outline stages, or classify types.
23. Research in which we examine numerical information from government documents or official reports so that we can address new research questions.
24. Research conducted on a set of people who share a common experience across time.
25. A type of applied research in which our purpose is to facilitate social change or a political-social goal.
26. Applied research in which we document the consequences for various areas of social life that are likely to result from introducing a major change in a community.
27. Research that takes place across several time points, in which we may look at different people or cases at in each time point.
28. Research into a topic area that has no one previously studied and in which we want to develop initial ideas and move toward a focused research question.
29. Any research in which we examine units or cases at more than one time point.
30. Information that is in the form of words, pictures, sounds, visual images, or objects.

Name _____

MATCHING KEY TERMS FOR CHAPTER 1

	Action-Oriented Research		Halo Effect
	Applied Research		Historical-Comparative Research
	Basic Research		Longitudinal Research
	Case-Study Research		Overgeneralization
	Cohort Analysis		Panel Study
	Cross-Sectional Research		Premature Closure
	Data		Qualitative Data
	Descriptive Research		Quantitative Data
	Empirical Evidence		Scientific Community
	Evaluation Research		Scientific Method
	Existing Statistics Research		Selective Observation
	Experimental Research		Social Impact Assessment
	Explanatory Research		Social Research
	Exploratory Research		Survey Research
	Field Research		Time Series Research

Name _____

Exercise 1.1

The president of Super Clean, Inc. is considering changing the firm's advertising to increase sales. She calls in the top management team to make a decision. The Vice President for Finance says, "New advertising was tried at Brightwhite, Inc., and it didn't work there so it won't work here." The Vice President for Human Resources says, "We can't change it because we've had the same advertising for the past 15 years, and it always worked OK before." The Vice President for Production says, "My brother is an expert on advertising, and he says it's a good idea." The Vice President for Marketing says, "I've read two articles in *National Business* on advertising, and they prove that the proposed new advertising is always best so we do not need to look any further.."

Which error of non-scientific thinking would be made if the President agreed with reasoning of the following? Use the following for your answers: Tradition, Authority, Media Myth, Premature Closure, Selective Observation, Overgeneralization. The reasoning of the Vice Presidents may have more than one error.

Vice President for Finance?
Explain your answer: Premature Closure - closing too soon
Overgeneralization - he has no proof it will not work
Selective Observation - he wants to do what he thinks

Vice President of Human Resources?
Explain your answer:
Tradition - he refuses to look beyond the past

Vice President of Production?
Explain your answer:
Authority - he has no basis for this assertion
Overgeneralization - "My brother does this therefore..."

Vice President for Marketing?
Explain your answer:
Selective Observation - he needs to read more and produce more
Premature Closure - too much conclusion just based on 2 articles
Media Myth - "National Business" may be biased

Name _____

Exercise 1.4

The top executives of Fast Airline Corporation were concerned sickness and missed work due to health problems among its employees who were heavy cigarette smokers. The Human Relations Department devised a quit-smoking program and asked Annabelle to conduct a study on the company's 16,000 employees. In January, she gave a survey questionnaire to each employee that asked about his or her smoking behavior and reactions to a planned program to reduce smoking. In the program, all non-smoking employees would get a $150 monthly reimbursement check from health savings for a period of three years if they continued to be non-smokers and had no smokers in their household. Each smoking employee could attend a two days quite smoking workshop and get full pay to attend.. They were also eligible to start the $150 monthly reimbursement after they had gone eight weeks without smoking at all. Once she surveyed all employees, Annabelle put the program into operation.

In June after the quit-smoking program had been in full operation, Annabelle conducted a second survey of all employees who had been working for the company in January. She again asked what they thought about it. As part of the survey, she asked persons who were smokers in January and who had taken advantage of the program whether they still smoked. In November all employees who had participated in the previous two surveys were surveyed for a third time. Annabelle again asked about their reactions to the program and about their smoking behavior. In December, Annabelle used the results for all three surveys to prepare a report for the Human Resources Department of Fast Airlines on how well the experimental program worked in reducing employee smoking.

1. Is Annabelle's research Exploratory, Descriptive or Explanatory?
   What about the description of the study tells you this?

2. Is Annabelle's research basic or applied?
   If applied, what type of applied is it? What in the description of the study tells you this?

3. Is the study cross-sectional, panel, time series or case study?
   What in the description of the study tells you this?

Name _____

Exercise 1.5

Go to your college library and look up three scholarly journal articles from the list below. Try to identify for each article, the Purpose (See Box 1.2, page 15 in the textbook), Time Dimension (See Figure 1.2, page 18 in the textbook) and Data Collection Technique (Pages 20-21 in the textbook). Write one-page explaining your answers and what specific features in the article told you that it is the type you have identified.

- Alpert, Geoffrey and others. 2005 "Police Suspicion And Discretionary Decision Making During Citizen Stops" *Criminology* pages 407-434.
- Bartholow, Bruce and others 2006 "Stereotype Activation and Control of Racial Bias" *Journal of Personality and Social Psychology* pages 272-287
- Clinton, Joshua and John Lapinski, 2004"Targeted" Advertising and Voter Turnout" *Journal of Politics* pages 69-96.
- Gavlee, Clarence C. 2005. "Ethnic classification in Southeastern Puerto Rico." *Social Forces* pages 949-970..
- Rose, Susan. 2005 "Going too Far? Sex, Sin and Social Policy." *Social Forces* pp 1207-1232.
- Savelsberg, Joachin and Ryan King. 2005 "Institutionalized Collective Memories of Hate." American *Journal of Sociology* pp. 579-616.
- Scott, Carter, J. Scott and Borch, Casey A" 2005. Assessing the Effects of Urbanism and Regionalism on Gender-Role Attitudes, 1974–1998" *Sociological Inquiry* pages 548-563
- Vilahdrich, Anahi 2005. "Tango Immigrants in New York City" *Journal of Contemporary Ethnography* pages 533-559

Article	Purpose	Time Dimension	Data Technique

CHAPTER 2

THEORY AND RESEARCH

LEARNING OBJECTIVES

After studying Chapter 2 you will be able to do the following:
1. Define social theory and describe how concepts are used in theory;
2. Distinguish between scientific and everyday explanations, prediction, and understanding;
3. Understand classifications and concept clusters in social theory;
4. Describe how theory and research complement one another;
5. Understand differences between micro, meso- and macro-levels of theorizing;
6. Distinguish between inductive and deductive directions of theory building;
7. Know the three main conditions for establishing causality;
8. Know differences among empirical generalizations, theory, and theoretical frameworks;
9. Understand the features of a causal, structural, and interpretative explanation.
10. Recognize key ideas of the three basic approaches to social research (positivist, interpretative, and critical).

KEY TERM MATCHING DEFINITIONS, CHAPTER 2

1. Complex, multidimensional concepts that have subtypes. They are parts of social theories between one simple concept and a full theoretical explanation.
2. A collection of closely connected ideas that refer to each other and are based on shared assumptions that all belong to the same social theory.
3. A co-occurrence of two events, factors, characteristics or activities, such that when one happens the other likely to occur as well. Many statistics measure this.
4. A statement in social theory about why events occur that is expressed in terms of causes and effects. They correspond to associations in the empirical world.
5. A statement about something that is likely to occur in the future.
6. A pure model about an idea, process or event. One develops it to think about it more clearly and systematically. It is used both as a method of qualitative data analysis and in social theory building.
7. Social theories and explanations about the concrete, small-scale and narrow level of reality, such as face-to-face interaction in small groups during a two-month period.
8. A quasi-theoretical statement that summarizes empirical regularities. It uses few abstract concepts and only makes a statement about a reoccurring pattern that researchers observe.

9. A basic statement in social theory that two ideas or variables are related to one another. It can be true or false (e.g., most sex offenders were themselves sexually abused when growing up), conditional (e.g., if a foreign enemy threatens, then the people of a nation will feel much stronger social solidarity), and/or causal (e.g., poverty causes crime).
10. Parts of social theories that are not tested, but are starting points or basic beliefs about the world. They are necessary to make other theoretical statements and to build social theory.
11. An approach to inquiry or social theory that begins with concrete empirical details, then works toward abstract ideas or principles.
12. Inductive social theory that is arises from and is closely rooted in specific empirical details.
13. An approach to inquiry or social theory in which one begins with abstract ideas and principles then works toward concrete, empirical details to test the ideas.
14. An association between two variables such that as values on variable increase, values on the other variable fall or decrease.
15. A type of social theory based on biological analogies, in which the social world and its parts are viewed as an intergrated system, with parts serving needs of the whole system.
16. A German word that translates as understanding, specifically it means an empathic understanding of another's worldview.
17. An approach based upon laws, or that operates according to a system of laws.
18. An approach that focuses on creating detailed descriptions of specific events in particular time periods and settings. It rarely goes beyond empirical generalizations to abstract social theory or causal laws.
19. An idea in critical social science that social theory and everyday practice interact or work together, mutually affecting one another. This interaction can promote social change. An action-oriented approach to social research.
20. A general organizing framework for social theory and empirical research. It includes basic assumptions, major questions to be answered, models of good research practice and theory, and methods for finding the answers to questions.
21. The principle that researchers must be able to repeat scientific findings in multiple studies to have a high level of confidence that the findings are true.
22. Social theories and explanations about the middle level of social reality between a broad and narrow scope, such as the development and operation of social organizations, communities, or social movements over a five-year period.
23. Social theories and explanations about more abstract, large-scale and broad-scope aspects of social reality, such as social change in major institutions (e.g., the family, education) in a whole nation across several decades.
24. An association between two variables such that as values on one increase, values on the other also increase.
25. A counterfeit argument presented as if it were a theoretical explanation. In it pointing to a responsible party for an unfavorable situation is substituted for presenting a causal explanation.

Name _____

MATCHING KEY TERMS FOR CHAPTER 2

	Association		Macro-Level
	Assumption		Meso-Level
	Blame Analysis		Micro-Level
	Causal Explanation		Negative Relationship
	Classification Concept		Nomothetic
	Concept Cluster		Paradigm
	Deductive Approach		Positive Relationship
	Empirical Generalization		Praxis
	Functional Theory		Prediction
	Grounded Theory		Proposition
	Ideal Type		Replication
	Idiographic		Verstehen
	Inductive Approach		

Name _____

Exercise 2.1

Develop a classification of types of college students. First, determine the purpose of the **classification**: Is it for a student who is seeking friends; for a professor organizing thinking about the students she/he encounters; for college administrators to plan for the needs of various types of students; for a residence hall director who wants to assign roommates; or for a recruiter looking for students for a job?

PURPOSE:

Next, decide upon one dimension of the classification (e.g., reasons students attend college, grades students get) and label at least three levels or categories of this dimension.

Decide on a second dimension of the classification and determine at least two levels or categories for this dimension.

Construct the classification by looking at the different combinations of students along the two dimensions. Label or give a name to each combination. You should have at least six types of students.

PRACTICE QUIZ 1, Chapters 1-2 (10 questions)

1. Which best describes the goal of **exploratory research**?

    a. Advance knowledge about an underlying process or complete a theory.
    b. Develop a better research question to ask and get a direction for future research.
    c. Give a verbal or numerical (e.g. percentages) picture.
    d. Extend a theory or principle into wholly new areas or issues.
    e. Provide evidence to support or refute an explanation.

2. What type of study examines a group of people who share a common life experience at the same time, then sees how that experience continues to have an impact on their behavior or attitudes?

    a. Cohort analysis
    b. Action-oriented research
    c. Cross-sectional research
    d. Field research
    e. Social Impact Assessment

3. All of the following characterize **applied research** EXCEPT which one?

    a. Doing research is usually part of a job assignment and sponsors/supervisors who are not professional researchers themselves will judge and use the findings.
    b. Success is based on whether sponsors/supervisors use the results in decision-making.
    c. The central goal is to produce practical payoffs or uses for the results.
    d. The research problems that one explores are limited by the interests of an employer or sponsor.
    e. The primary concern is with the internal logic and rigor of the research design, so a researcher attempts to reach the very highest levels of scientific rigor and quality of scholarship.

4. In 2006 Professor Dennis Wu conducted a study of 1,000 African American persons who were married in 1962-1963 and are still married. He believed that the social-political climate around the early phase of the 1960s Civil Rights movement (1960-1966) affected their decision to marry and shaped decisions in their first years of marriage. Most likely, he was conducting what type of study?

    a. case study
    b. panel
    c. cohort
    d. time series
    e. cross-sectional

5. Three major approaches or paradigms in social research were introduced, positivist, interpretative, and critical. If someone adopted the **critical approach**, which of the following would they be most likely to agree with?

   a. Social research should be value-free and precisely measure aspects of the social world, and use statistics.
   b. Social researchers should test causal theories and replicate results.
   c. Social research should focus on the ideas, subjective beliefs, motives, and perceptions that people hold about reality, and not try to capture "objective" reality.
   d. Social researchers should begin by stripping away the surface level of reality that contains illusion and falsehoods. Instead of being value free, researchers should take an activist stand and try to change the world and advance social justice.
   e. Social researchers should try to gain an empathetic understanding of the worldview of people being studied. Instead of trying to copy the natural sciences, social researchers should build on how people live, which is by constructing social meanings through social interaction.

6. In Chapter 1 you learned the seven steps process of doing research. In addition to the seven steps, the diagram of them showed a circle in the center of the sequence of steps that had an influence on how a researcher conducted each step. What was in that circle?

   a. Qualitative vs. quantitative data
   b. Halo effect
   c. Time dimension in research
   d. Social Theory
   e. Causality

7. If a James Jorgstog says that he will follow an **inductive approach**, what does that mean?

   a. He will begin with highly abstract ideas and work toward observing very concrete data.
   b. He will begin with observing very concrete data and work toward highly abstract ideas.
   c. He will use a causal explanation that is unidirectional and predicts a positive relationship.
   d. He will begin with a paradigm, then select a theory, then select propositions, and finally gather the data.

8. You learned many terms related to social theory in Chapter 2. If you were to rank order them from the broadest and most abstract at one end, to the narrowest, most specific and concrete at the other end, which term would be at the **narrowest, most specific** and concrete end?

    a. Paradigm
    b. Empirical generalization
    c. Theoretical framework
    d. Middle-range theory

9. Verstehen basically means

    a. Voluntarism
    b. Understanding
    c. Replication
    d. Relativism
    e. Inductive

10. Kieko Kamakura wants to create a **nomothetic explanation**. This means that she will:

    a. Try to create an explanation that is cross-sectional.
    b. Try to create an explanation that only has positive relationships in the theory.
    c. Try to create an explanation that uses grounded theory.
    d. Try to create an explanation based on detailed specifics of a particular case.
    e. Try to create an explanation that is expressed in terms of general laws.

CHAPTER 3

ETHICS IN SOCIAL RESEARCH

LEARNING OBJECTIVES

After studying Chapter 3 you will be able to do the following
1. Understand the historical development of a concern for ethics in social research and its origins in specific events;
2. Discuss dilemmas or issues involved in the treatment of human subjects;
3. Understand the pressures on researchers who conduct sponsored research and debate ways to respond to such pressures;
4. Explain the role of an IRB and informed consent requirements;
5. Describe the role of a code of professional ethics and the types of items found in them;

KEY TERMS MATCHING DEFINITIONS, CHAPTER 3

1. A statement, usually written, in which people in a study learn aspects about the project and formally agree to participate.
2. A type of unethical behavior in which a researcher fakes or creates false data, or falsely reports on the research procedure.
3. When one 'steals' the ideas or writings of another or uses them without citing the source.
4. The ethical protection for those who are studied of holding research data in confidence or keeping them secret from the public; not releasing information in a way that permits linking specific individuals to specific responses. Researchers do this by only presenting data in an aggregate form (e.g., percentages, means, etc.).
5. The ethical protection that the people studied remain nameless; their identity is protected from disclosure and remains unknown.
6. A committee at colleges, hospitals, and research institutes that is required by federal law to ensure that research involving humans is conducted in a responsible, ethical manner.
7. A person who sees ethical wrongdoing, tries to correct it internally but then informs an external audience, agency or the media.
8. When someone engages in <u>research fraud</u>, <u>plagiarism</u>, or other unethical conduct that significantly deviates from the accepted practice for conducting and reporting research within the <u>scientific community</u>.
9. An ethical principle that people should never participate in research unless they first explicitly agree to do so.

Student Workbook for Neuman, *Basics of Social Research*, 2e   19

10. A type of <u>experimental design</u> in which all groups receive the <u>treatment</u> so that discomfort or benefits are shared and inequality is not created.
11. People who lack the necessary cognitive competency give real <u>informed consent</u> or people in a weak position that might comprise their freedom to refuse to participate in a study.
12. An approach to social research in which a researcher tries to enrich public debate over moral or political issues by infusing them with social theory and social research findings.

MATCHING KEY TERMS FOR CHAPTER 3

	Anonymity		Principle of Voluntary Consent
	Confidentiality		Public Sociology
	Cross-over Design		Research Fraud
	Informed Consent		Scientific Misconduct
	Institutional Review Board (IRB)		Special Population
	Plagiarism		Whistleblower

Exercise 3.1

Find out about your college's or university IRB. If it does not have one, ask your teacher to explain why it does not. If it does, answer or do each of the following:

1. Who are members of the IRB? Give each person's name and title/occupation.

2. How often does it meet to review research proposals?

3. Obtain a copy of a form used to submit proposals and attach it.

4. Obtain a copy of an informed consent form and attach it.

5. Sit in on a meeting and write a 1–2 page description of the meeting and issues discussed at it.

Name _____

Exercise 3.2

On the CD with this book, go to Chapter 3 and locate a copy of the Code of Ethics for two social science associations. Select one of the following:

- American Anthropology Association,
- American Political Science Association,
- American Psychological Association
- American Sociological Association,
- American Association for Public Opinion Research
- National Association of Social Workers

Compare the two codes regarding issues of informed consent and confidentiality. Attach a copy of each new code of ethics and write a two-page essay discussing the similarities and differences between two.

Exercise 3.3

Role play the following situation on videotape or live before the class. Mr. or Ms. X has worked for Research Data, Inc. for six months conducting social research. X thinks s/he is doing a good job and has a chance to build a well-paying, secure career at Research Data, Inc. This is important to X because such jobs are difficult to come by. One day, Mr. Z, who is X's supervisor, comes into X's office and closes the door. In a serious tone, Mr. Z asks X to "adjust" the sampling frame and change five questions in a survey that will be conducted by Research Data, Inc. for Big Banana, Inc. The original sampling frame included grocery stores all across North America, but Mr. Z wants to drop seven areas where few bananas are sold. Mr. Z wants the questions on the questionnaire modified to increase estimates of future banana purchases and show a strong desire of consumers for bananas. Mr. Z said that this will make the market for Big Banana, Inc. look much better. Strong results will help Big Banana get the $15 million bank loan it needs for plant expansion. Mr. Z says that Research Data, Inc. regularly gets large contracts from Big Banana, Inc. and he does not want to lose the account to a competing research firm. He also says all research firms do this type of modification, and no one will get hurt. There is a hidden threat in the request: X's future career at Research Data depends on X being a "team player" who understands the needs of the company. Also, if business drops at Research Data, X will be first on the layoff list. If X proves to be a loyal employee who does what s/he is told on an important account, his/her future at Research Data, Inc. looks much better. The only problem is that Mr. Z's request is unethical.

Name _____

Exercise 3.4

Go to the CD that accompanies this Workbook go to Chapter 3. Locate the sites for On Being a Scientist by NATIONAL ACADEMY OF SCIENCES (U.S) and Office for Human Research Protections by DEPARTMENT OF HEALTH AND HUMAN SERVICES (U.S.)

Read the following sections of it:

- Social Foundations of Science,
- Values in Science, Allocation of Credit
- Misconduct in Science
- Responding to Violations.

Select one of the following names/terms put it in an Internet Search engine (such as Google) for one of the following four famous studies in Human Subject Protection.

- Laud Humphreys, Tearoom Trade
- Stanley Milgram, Obedience Study
- Philip Zimbardo Prison Study
- Bad Blood

Review the discussion of the case that you found and attach a print out of a web page.

Now write a 2-page essay that explains the specific ethical guidance or prohibitions that are now provided by the On Being a Scientist report and statements by the Office for Human Research Protection that would have helped to prevent the abuses in the famous study if they had been in place at the time the famous case occurred.

CHAPTER 4

REVIEWING THE SCHOLARLY LITERATURE AND PLANNING A STUDY

LEARNING OBJECTIVES

After studying Chapter 4 you will be able to do the following:
1. Conduct a literature review using location tools designed for that purpose.
2. Correctly write a bibliographic citation for a scholarly journal using the ASR format.
3. Understand the benefits and limits of the Internet for social research;
4. Understand variables and be able to identify independent, dependent, and intervening variables;
5. Identify and create a hypothesis with the characteristics of causal hypotheses;
6. Understand the *logic of the disconfirming hypothesis* and its relation to the *null hypothesis*;
7. Understand *units of analysis* and be able to apply the idea in specific situations;
8. Recognize the *ecological fallacy, reductionism,* and *spuriousness* in a specific situation and understand why they are not good causal hypotheses;
9. Take a general topic and narrow it down into a highly specific research question and hypothesis, stating the variables and direction of causality;
10. Recognize differences between qualitative and quantitative research design.

KEY TERM MATCHING DEFINITIONS, CHAPTER 4

1. The kind of empirical case or unit that a researcher observes, measures and analyzes in a study.
2. The categories or levels of a variable.
3. The first variable that causes or produces the effect in a causal explanation.
4. A variable that is between the initial causal variable and the final effect variable in a causal explanation.
5. The broad class of units that are covered in a hypothesis. All the units to which the findings of a specific study might be generalized.
6. A statement that appears to be a causal explanation, but is not because a hidden, unmeasured or initially unseen variable. The unseen variable comes earlier in the temporal order, and it has a causal impact on the what was initially posited to be the independent variable as well as the dependent variable.
7. A way to talk about the scope of a social theory, causal explanation, proposition, hypothesis or theoretical statement. The range of phenomena it covers or to which it applies, from social psychological, micro-level, to organizational, meso-level, to large-scale social structure, macro-level.

8. A hypothesis that says there is no relationship or association between two variables, or no effect.
9. The effect variable that is last and results from the causal variable(s) in a causal explanation. Also the variable that is measured in the pretest and posttest, and that is the result of the treatment in experimental research.
10. Something that appears to be a causal explanation, but is not. It occurs because of a confusion about units of analysis. A researcher has empirical evidence about an association for large-scale units or huge aggregates, but overgeneralizes to make theoretical statements about an association among small-scale units or individuals.
11. Something that appears to be a causal explanation, but is not because of a confusion about units of analysis. A researcher has empirical evidence for an association at the level of individual behavior or very small-scale units, but overgeneralizes to make theoretical statements about very large-scale units.
12. The statement from a causal explanation or a proposition that has at least one independent and one dependent variable, but it has yet to be empirically tested.
13. A term with two meanings in literature reviews: a short summary of a scholarly journal article that usually appears at its beginning, and a reference tool for locating scholarly journal articles.
14. Details of a scholarly journal article's location that helps people to find it quickly.
15. A hypothesis paired with a null hypothesis stating that the independent variable has an effect on a dependent variable.
16. A type of concept or construct, or its empirical indicator, that has two or more categories, levels or values.
17. Research that proceeds in a clear, logical, step-by-step straight line. It is more characteristic of a quantitative than a qualitative approach to social research.
18. Research that proceeds in a circular, back-and-forth manner. It is more characteristic of a qualitative than a quantitative style to social research.
19. In qualitative research, what the people who are being studied actually feel and think.
20. In qualitative research, what a researcher believes the people being studied feel and think.
21. In qualitative research, what a researcher tells the reader of a research report that the people he or she studied felt and thought.
22. A systematic examination of previously published studies on a research question, issue, or method that a researcher undertakes and integrates together to prepare for conducting a study or to bring together and summarize the "state of the field."

Name _____

MATCHING TERMS FOR CHAPTER 4

13	Abstract	17	Linear Research Path
15	Alternate Hypothesis	22	Literature Review
2	Attributes	18	Non-Linear Research Path
14	Citation	8	Null Hypothesis
9	Dependent Variable	11	Reductionism
10	Ecological Fallacy	20	Second Order Interpretation
19	First Order Interpretation	6	Spuriousness
12	Hypothesis	21	Third-Order Interpretation
3	Independent Variable	1	Unit of Analysis
4	Intervening Variable	3	Universe
7	Level of Analysis	16	Variable

Student Workbook for Neuman, *Basics of Social Research*, 2e   25

Name _____

Exercise 4.1

Part 1: The four case studies below has each of the following five problems and one has nothing wrong with it: **Ecological Fallacy, Reductionism, Spuriousness, or Nothing wrong.** Match the problem (or nothing wrong) to the appropriate case. Put X in the box below.

Part 2: For each of the cases identify the **independent and dependent variables**.

Check a box Indicating which error goes with which case.	**CASE 1 Rubber Tires**	**CASE 2 Drunk Drivers**	**CASE 3 Homeless Children**	**CASE 4 Gentrification**
Ecological Fallacy				
Reductionism				
Spuriousness				
Nothing Wrong				
Write in the variables and unit of analysis for each case in the space	**CASE 1 Rubber Tires**	**CASE 2 Drunk Drivers**	**CASE 3 Homeless Children**	**CASE 4 Gentrification**
Independent Variables				
Dependent Variables				
Unit of Analysis				

CASE 1: RUBBER TIRES, Inc.

In early 2005, the Vice President for Human Resource of Rubber Tires, Inc. developed a new vacation/leave program for employees. He asked Assistant Manager Maria Lopez to evaluate how employees felt about the vacation/leave program and their level of satisfaction with it. To do her research Maria went to the administration department of Rubber Tires where she gathered information on each of the company's 100 plants in various world-wide locations. For each plant she gathered information on the number of vacation and leave days, cost of the program, and the average productivity and absentee rates for each month for one year. Mary found that the program cost was over $250,000 a year at 40 plants. At these plants the absentee rate was 10 percent and productivity was 1600 tires per worker per month. At another 40 plants, the program cost was $150,000 or less per year. For the low cost plants the absentee rate was 12 percent and production was 1200 tires per month. The remaining 20 plants had program costs of between $150,000 and $250,000, and an absentee rate of 16 per cent and a production rate of 1500 tires per month. Maria reasoned that high cost programs produced low absentee rates and high productivity rates. Plants with a low cost program also had a low absentee rate, but much lower productivity rate. Maria's report concluded that the employees found the program to be valuable and were highly satisfied with it. She recommended continuing the program because so many of the employees who used the program were happy workers.

CASE 2: DRUNK DRIVERS OF WOODSBURNING

Police chief Schultz of the town of Woodsburning in Queensland, Australia studied drunk driving by looking at arrest records of various police agencies and traveling with drunk driver police patrols. He interviewed police officers and examined statistics. After a year of research, he thought he uncovered the reason for drunk driving. Chief Schultz discovered that a majority of the people that the police had arrested for drunk driving had a particular personality type. They were high risk-takers. These people took risks in other areas of their lives. He confirmed this hypothesis by conducting personality tests on 1,000 people in six nearby towns between the ages of 18 and 40 who had been arrested for drunk driving. He also conducted tests on 1,000 similar people who police had never arrested for drunk driving. He found that those who police had arrested for drunk driving were much more likely to have a risk-taking personality. These people got a sense of excitement or a thrill from experiencing high risk, and they blocked thinking about negative consequences. Such people were more likely to engage in other high risk behaviors (e.g., enjoy high risk sports, never wear seat belts, gamble, smoke, etc.), than those who police had never arrested for drunk driving. He found that some people's personality makes them less sensitive to bad events caused by their behavior. These are the people who are more likely to drink and drive. As a further check, the chief asked all 2,000 people whether they thought driving after drinking was risky. He found that 85 percent of both groups agreed that drinking then driving was risky. The risk-taking people were not as worried that something (e.g., arrest, an accident) would happen to them. People with a particular type of personality were more willing to take a chance, because they felt a need for excitement and felt lucky.

CASE 3: HOMELESS CHILDREN

JoAnn Guo studied battered women for her senior honor's thesis in social work. She wanted to explain why homeless families with children had learning problems. She went to the library and read extensively on the topic. Cindy discovered that homeless adults with children were more likely to have poor nutrition and move frequently. She also found that the have adults were likely to emotional disorders-mental illnesses and difficulty finding regular work with decent pay. With emotional or mental disorders and no money, they often moved and did not follow nutritional guidelines. Other research studies she read suggested that homeless children are likely to have emotional disorders-mental illnesses and difficulty finding regular work when they become adults. In addition, emotional and mental disorder and poverty inhibit learning. She also read that people whose parents had emotional disorders or mental illness when they were children are more likely to have similar problems as adults. This is because of generic transmission, few mental health services, and poor coping skills. After summarizing the literature, Cindy concluded that the real cause of homeless children having learning problems there parents did not have a eating habits and did not stay put. She thought that if only the parents ate properly and were not allowed to move, the children's learning would improve. She reasoned social workers should encourage the good eating and not moving, then the problem of children with learning problems would end.

CASE 4: GENTRIFICATION

Dr. My Bigtoe studied the development of gentrification in major Texas cities between 1985 and 2005. He noticed that center city districts of most cities had gentrification, i.e., the building of new housing and shopping areas for upper-middle income people. The number of professionals rose, and they bought up housing or renovated housing that previously was used by low-income people. The low income people were forced to move. During the two decades, many new shopping areas, new condos and expensive apartments appeared. In addition, private schools and expensive shops for high income people increased. Low income people had to relocate to other parts of the city, ended up paying more in rent, and often their children had to switch schools. Traditional local neighborhood institutions in low income neighborhoods, i.e., the churches, local shops, barber shops, low cost bars and restaurants, clubs, etc. often went out of business. Dr. Bigtoe discovered a government bureaucrat in the Texas Department of Urban Development and Housing Construction, Henry Wiseman. Mr. Wiseman had been assigned the task of preparing a program to limit rapid, excessive gentrification in 1984. Unfortunately, Mr. Wiseman had a bad back and was on medical leave for 20 years. During his absence, no one else was assigned to his task. In 2003, two years after he returned to work, he slipped on a banana at lunch and accidentally hit a button which destroyed all his work that had been stored in a computer. He also again hurt his back and took another medical leave. Dr. Bigtoe said that due to circumstances of Mr. Wiseman, the Texas government failed to respond to the problem of excessive gentrification. Dr. Bigtoe concluded that the cause of Texas urban gentrification was the misfortune of Henry Wiseman. If only Henry not hurt his back and had done his job, the problem of widespread gentrification in Texas cities would not be with us today.

Name _____

Exercise 4.2

Identify the <u>Unit of Analysis,</u> <u>Universe</u> and <u>Dependent Variable</u> in each of the eight condensed summaries of articles below. You may wish to go to the library and read them, but there is sufficient information here.

1. In "The Effects of Visual Images in Political Ads: Experimental Testing of Distortions and Visual Literacy " (*Social Science Quarterly* 2000 81:913-27) Gary Noggle and Lynda Kaid used experimental methods to compare distorted and non-distorted political advertising. Distorted ads used video editing techniques to give a false impression, special effects, or false imagery. For example, the ad had a false background or false audience before a candidate, or elements of an actual scene were "erased" to create a positive impression. Some people say television viewers are sophisticated with "visual literacy," and few are fooled by the tactics. The experiment was done twice, once with 250 individuals recruited from classes at a university were randomly divided in half, and six months later with 200 individuals from another university. One half of subjects saw distorted ads and one half saw non-distorted ads. The ads were selected from ones actually used but in a different part of the country. Subjects were asked to evaluate the candidate and whether they would vote for the candidate in the ad or the opponent. Results showed that subjects were favorable to candidates in distorted ads and more likely to vote for the candidate, even among subjects who were more sophisticated in their use of media. The authors conclude that increased distortion in political ads is probably working for candidates who use them to manipulate voters.

2. In "The Politics of Bilingual Education Expenditures in Urban Districts." (*Social Science Quarterly* 2000 81:1064-72) David Leal and Fred Hess examined the political, demographic and fiscal determinants of urban school district spending on bilingual education in the United States. They used data from a survey of all school boards in the U.S. They combined school board survey information with census information on the school district. In order to measure the amount spend on bilingual education, they divided all spending on bilingual education by number of pupils to get per-pupil spending on bilingual education in each district. They found that districts with more Latinos on the school board, even in districts with equal numbers of Latino children, the more was spent for bilingual education. A similar positive effect was found for Asians on the school board, but not for blacks or women on the board.

3. In "Atheists as 'Other'" (*American Sociological Review* 2006 71:211-234) Penny Edgell, Joseph Gerteis and Douglas Hartmann studied American's attitudes toward atheists. They used data from a telephone survey of Americans in 2003 and 2004. They found that rejection of atheists generally and as a martial partner for a son or daughter was stronger than for any other social or religious group. The people who were most negative toward atheists tended to be highly religious people who said diversity was not an important value and who did not emphasize that government should protect the rights of all people. Based on in-depth interviews and other information, the authors suggest that atheists play more of symbolic role as someone who rejects membership in American cultural and social life.

4. In "Political Culture in Canada and the United States: Comparing Social Trust, Self-Esteem, and Political Liberalism" (*Social Science Quarterly* 2000: 81:826-36) David Moon,

Nicholas Lovrich, and John Pierce examined the political cultures in the cities of Canada and the United States. They pulled together many different types of data to create measures of social trust, self-esteem, and liberalism in 7 Canadian and 47 US cities. They wanted to find out whether with increased media and other communication across the border, whether U.S. and Canada maintain distinct political cultures and have different social values. Although they did not include every city in each country, they conclude, "Canadians in these cities are substantially higher in social trust and somewhat higher in self-esteem than residents in the United States." For both these measures, the differences existed at all age levels. Political liberalism differences were also found. In the U.S., younger people were most liberal while in Canada, it was the older generation.

5. In "Social Isolation in America: Changes in Core Discussion Networks over Two Decades" *American Sociological Review* 2006 71:353-375) Miller McPherson, Lynn Smith-Lovin and Matthew Brashears examined what individual Americans reported about the number of other people they talked with, both family and non-family. The authors created a measure of individual social networks in 1985 and 2004. They found that the size of discussion networks declined; in short, Americans are talking to fewer other people. Over time, people were more likely to talk to others who have a similar educational background but people of more diverse racial-ethnic backgrounds. Social contacts narrowed: fewer with neighbors and voluntary associations declined and more with spouses or parents.

6. In "White Ethnic Diversity and Community Attachment in Small Iowa Towns" (*Social Science Quarterly* 2001 82:397-407) Tom Rice and Brent Steele looked at the relationship between white ethnic diversity and community attachment in 99 small Iowa towns. They developed a "community attachment" score for each town based on interviews and census data that measured ethnic diversity. They found that more ethnically diverse towns had lower levels of community attachment. In addition, more diverse towns showed higher levels of suspicion and lower levels of trust than ethnically homogeneous towns.

7. In the "Treadmill of Destruction" (2004, *American Sociological Review* 69:558-575) Greg Hooks and Chad L. Smith tested a theory in environmental sociology called the "Treadmill of Destruction" by looking at the location of closed military bases with none to many high risk unexploded ordinance (i.e., bullets, bombs, shells, etc). The found information on such closed bases in all 3,100 counties in the 48 continental United States. According to the "Treadmill of Destruction" high risk environmental hazards would be located relatively powerless people. The authors then checked whether countries had Native American lands. Consistent with the theory, the found that high risk sites tended to be located on or close to Native American land.

8. In "Defended Neighborhoods, Integration and Racially Motivated Crime" (*American Journal of Sociology* 1998, 104:372-403) Donald Green, Dara Strolovitch and Janelle Wong examined anti-minority crimes in New York City. They attempted to explain the number of crimes directed against Asians, Latinos and blacks. New York City created a Bias Crime Unit in 1981 that collects data on crimes in which the prejudice against a victim's race, religion, ethnicity, or sexual orientation was a motivation. Data was available on 59 "community districts," which are used by city agencies to represent neighborhoods, and authors gathered other information on characteristics on each district. The authors found no relationship between economic conditions (e.g., unemployment) in a district and crime, but found strong effects of the in-migration by minorities into districts that were predominately white on such crimes. More racially integrated neighborhoods had a lower rate of such crimes. The authors conclude with a discussion of actions by people to keep one's neighborhood racially homogenous defending and one's "turf" against outsider groups as a source of crime.

Article	Unit of Analysis	Universe	Dependent Variable
1			
2			
3			
4			
5			
6			
7			
8			

Name _____

Exercise 4.3

On the CD with this book, go to Chapter 1 to locate 4 scholarly articles that published after January 1, 2002 on the same topic. The articles must come from one of the following academic journals:

American Behavioral Scientist
American Journal of Sociology
American Sociological Review
Criminology
Gender and Society
Journal of Marriage and Family
Journal of Politics
Social Forces
Social Problems
Social Science Quarterly
Sociological Forum
Sociological Inquiry
Sociological Quarterly
Sociological Perspectives
Sociological Spectrum
Sociology Journal

On the CD with this book, go to Chapter 4 to review the ASA style. Prepare a bibliography in ASA style. Use only articles from scholarly journals that report on empirical research (NOT theoretical essays or book reviews). Follow the ASA style exactly.

Exercise 4.4

Below is a list of six studies on the topic, Attitudes about the victims of rape published between 1995 and 2005. Locate and read the four of the articles. Write a three-page literature review synthesizing the findings of the articles. Explain how the dependent variable, attitude toward the victims of rape, was measured. Also discuss the major independent variables examined that include general role beliefs, race/ethnicity gender, and professional background.

Campbell, Rebecca and Sheela Raja. 2005. "The Sexual Assault and Secondary Victimization of Female Veterans." Psychology of Women Quarterly. 29:97-106.

Mori, Lisa and Jeffrey Bernat.1995. "Attitude Toward Rape: Gender and Ethnic Differences Across Asian and Caucasian College Students" Sex Roles 32:457-468.

Wakelin, Anna and Karen Long. 2003. "Effects of Victim Gender and Sexuality on Attributions of Blame to Rape Victims." Sex Roles 49:477-487.

Whatley, Mark. 2005. "The Effect of Participant Sex, Victim Dress, and Traditional Attitudes on Causal Judgments for Marital Rape Victims." Journal of Family Violence; 20:191–200.

White, Bradley H. and Sjarpm Robinson Kurpius. 1999. "Attitudes Toward Rape Victims" Journal of Interpersonal Violence 14:989-996.

Xenos, Sophia and David Smith, David. 2001. "Perceptions of Rape and Sexual Assault Among Australian Adolescents and Young Adults" Journal of Interpersonal Violence 16: 1103–1120.

Name _____

Exercise 4.5

Go to your college library and ask a librarian how to use the interlibrary loan service. Check out an interlibrary loan book for a book that your college library does not have.

1. Give the citation for the book you borrowed. Follow the citation system for the *American Sociological Association*:

2. How did you find out that the book was not in your library, but was available elsewhere?

3. Where did the interlibrary loan book come from? _____
   How long did it take to arrive? _____
   How long can you borrow it? _____

4. Ask a librarian about all the various computerized search services that are available for finding books and articles on a social science topic. List them.

5. Conduct a search using *Sociological Abstracts* or *Sociofile*. Select a topic and list six keywords you will give the librarian: using keywords which you developed from your topic.

   _____ _____

   _____ _____

   _____ _____

6. Conduct the search for all languages and all articles published after 1997.
   How many items were found? _____
   How many items were not in English? _____

7. Conduct a second search for English-only articles published after 2001.
   How many items were found? _____

8. How many of the items located by the search are NOT available in your local college library? _____
   Explain how you found this out:

Name _____

PRACTICE QUIZ 2, Chapters 3–4 (18 questions)

1. Professor Davis's results will be reported where most scientific research first appears. Where is this?

    a. Television news
    b. Newspapers
    c. Newsmagazines
    d. Scholarly journals
    e. College textbooks

2. Which of the following would **NOT** be considered as a "special population" for social research purposes?

    a. A group of eight-year old children.
    b. A random sample of adults at a shopping mall.
    c. The prisoners at a state prison.
    d. Students in an introduction to sociology class.
    e. Homeless people at a shelter.

3. What information that is provided in an ASA citation but is ABSENT from this description of a scholarly journal article?

    The article appeared in 2003 in issue 3 of *Social Behavior and Personality*. "Mock Juror Ratings of Guilt in Canada " was written by Jeffrey Pfeifer (Department of Psychology, Regina University in Saskatchewan, Canada) and James Ogloff (Centre for Social Change and Social Equity, Monash University, Queensland, Australia). It is part of a larger study on funded by the Social Sciences and Research Council of Canada.

    a. date
    b. page numbers
    c. volume number
    d. publication title
    e. b and c

4. Which is the principle of ethics was probably seriously violated in the situation described below?

People who go to a drug treatment center to get help for heroin addiction are told that they can volunteer to become subjects in a study on a new treatment, but they will not be told whether they are in the control or experimental group. The volunteers are randomly divided into two groups. One group of volunteers receives a placebo (no drug at all) and the other group receives a drug which previous research has shown to be highly effective in reducing heroin dependency. After one year in the study, the researcher compares the two groups for heroin dependency.

   a. Do not cause physical harm to subjects
   b. Do not create unnecessary psychological stress or anxiety
   c. Do not place subject in legal jeopardy
   d. Protect the confidentiality of subjects
   e. Do not create new inequalities

5. We can learn about ethics based "famous cases." Which study is the "famous case" in which college students were used in a very life-like experiment. Unexpectedly, the subjects became highly involved in the roles of the experiment. Realizing that the subjects had lost perspective and forgot they were in an experiment and fearing they could be harmed, the researcher ended the experiment one week early. The principle to protect the subjects from harm took precedence over the need to complete the experiment.

   a. Humphrey's Tearoom Trade
   b. Sir Cyril Burt's studies of twins
   c. Milgram Obedience Experiment
   d. Zimbardo Prison Experiment
   e. Bad Blood

6. Survey researcher, Slim Slime, telephones respondents and lies by telling them he is from "University Opinion Research." He gives no other identifying information; he does not tell them that the survey is voluntary or what it is about, but immediately asks personal questions. The respondents never learn who Mr. Slime really was. Afterwards, Mr. Slime gives a market research company each respondent's name and address attached to their answers to questions. What ethical principle(s) has he violated?

   a. Failing to get informed consent
   b. Breach of confidentiality
   c. Inappropriate use of deception
   d. All of the above
   e. None of the above; this is standard practice and is ethical.

7. An informed consent statement would **NOT** include:

   a. How much money it costs the researcher to conduct the study
   b. A guarantee of anonymity and confidentiality
   c. A description of the procedure of the study
   d. A statement that participation is completely voluntary
   e. All are included

8. If you wanted to locate the most empirical studies directly related to education and schools, which specialized literature searching tool would be best?

   a. Sociological Abstracts
   b. Social Science Citation Index
   c. ERIC
   d. Reader's Guide
   e. Current Contents

9. Ken Clark wanted to test the hypothesis: "White males who strongly oppose gun control laws and who own pistols are more likely to be racially prejudiced towards blacks than are white males who favor gun control laws and who do not own pistols." His **dependent variable** is:

   a. Gun ownership
   b. White males
   c. Racial prejudice towards blacks
   d. Gun control laws
   e. Insufficient information provided

10. Which of the following sets are **variables**?

    a. Female, Catholic, educational level
    b. Plumber, professor, dentist
    c. Occupation, political party preference, divorce rate
    d. 22 years old, married, income level
    e. None of the above

11. A researcher conducted a study of women's attitudes toward raising the tax on cigarettes. Her **unit of analysis** are:

    a. Individual women
    b. Attitudes
    c. Cigarettes
    d. Taxes
    e. None of the above

12. A researcher examined newspaper editorials from 20 major U.S. cities that dealt with the topic of grade inflation in high schools. The **unit of analysis** was

   a. Grade Inflation
   b. Major cities
   c. Newspapers
   d. Newspaper editorials
   e. High Schools

13. Juanita, a qualitative researcher, interprets what she sees in a setting and brings some preliminary coherence to observations by putting them in a context of a stream of events. This is called,

   a. First order interpretation
   b. Second order interpretation
   c. Third order interpretation

Use the following model for question 14

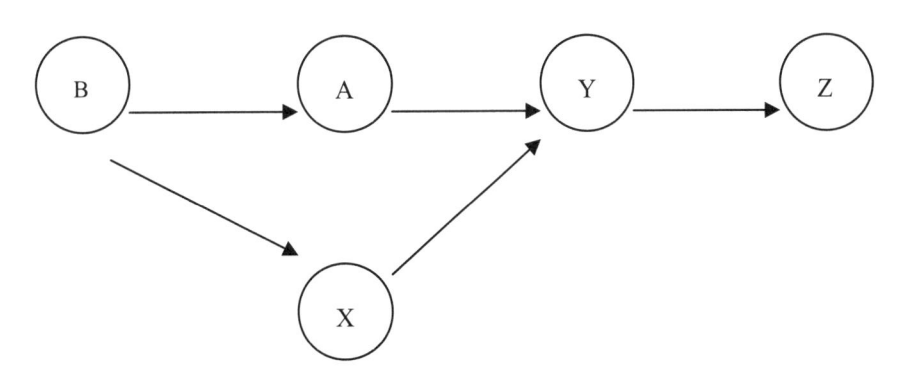

14. The **dependent variable** is symbolized by:
   a. X
   b. Z
   c. Z
   d. A
   e. B

use for 15 to 18

David Jacobs and Marc Dixon (2006 "The Politics of Labor-Management Relations" Social Problems 53:118-137) examined the passage of "Right –To-Work" laws in 50 states of the United States between 1960 and 1990. These state laws greatly influence the ability of workers to form or join labor unions and the ability of employers control relations in the workplace. The authors thought that the laws were the outcome of political struggles between pro-labor and pro-management forces. Their data came from the *Statistical Abstract of the United States.* The authors looked at pro-labor and pro-management conditions and the laws in each state. Pro-management factors included many small-scale businesses, citizens who expressed conservative beliefs, and a high percent of African Americans. A high percent of African Americans weakens pro-labor forces because the historically American labor movement has been divided along racial lines.

15. In this study, the **dependent variable** is:

    a. labor unions
    b. whether a state had a Right-to-Work law
    c. 50 states
    d. Statistical Abstract of the United States
    e. percent of African Americans

16. In this study, two **independent variables** are:

    a. percent of African Americans and small businesses
    b. Right-to-Work law and conservative political beliefs by citizens
    c. 50 states and Right-to-Work law
    d. 50 states and Statistical Abstract of the United States

17. In this study, the **universe** is:

    a. all laws
    b. Statistical Abstract of the United States
    c. African Americans
    d. labor unions
    e. the states of the United States

18. In this study, the **unit of analysis** is:

    a. the law
    b. the state
    c. the individual citizen
    d. the African American
    e. the data source (Statistical Abstract of the United States)

Student Workbook for Neuman, *Basics of Social Research*, 2e 39

CHAPTER 5

QUALITATIVE AND QUANTITATIVE MEASUREMENT

LEARNING OBJECTIVES

After studying Chapter 5 you will be able to do the following:
1. Describe the measurement process and how to move from an abstract construct to a specific indicator;
2. Explain the role of conceptualization and operationalization, and develop conceptual and operational definitions for variables.
3. Explain how conceptual and empirical hypothesis differ.
4. Contrast quantitative and qualitative approaches to conceptualization and operationalization;
5. Define the idea of reliability.
6. Define measurement validity, distinguish it from other types of validity;
7. Explain major types of measurement validity;
8. Discuss the four levels of measurement, differences among them, and identify the level of a specific indicator;
9. Understand the purpose and uses of standardization, indexes and scaling in social measurement;
10. Explain how unidimensionality and mutually exclusive and exhaustive categories are used in scale and index construction.

KEY TERMS MATCHING DEFINITIONS, CHAPTER 5

1. How well an empirical indicator and the conceptual definition of the construct that the indicator is supposed to measure "fit" together.
2. The dependability or consistency of the measure of a variable.
3. The procedure to statistically adjust measures to permit making an honest comparison by giving a common basis to measures of different units.
4. A type of measurement validity in which an indicator "makes sense" as a measure of a construct in the judgment of others, especially those in the scientific community.
5. The process developing a clear, rigorous, systematic conceptual definitions for abstract ideas/concepts.
6. The process of moving from the conceptual definition of a construct to a set of specific activities or measures that allow a researcher to observe it empirically, i.e., its operational definition.
7. A type of hypothesis in which the researcher expresses variables in abstract, conceptual terms and expresses the relationship among variables in a theoretical way.
8. A type of hypothesis in which the researcher expresses variables in specific empirical terms and expresses the association among the measured indicators in observable, empirical terms.
9. The principle that when using multiple indicators to measure a construct, all the

indicators should consistently fit together and indicate a single construct.
10. A system that organizes the information in the measurement of variables into four general levels, from nominal-level to ratio-level.
11. The lowest, least precise level of measurement for which there is only a difference in type among the categories of a variable.
12. The highest, most precise level of measurement for which variable attributes can be rank ordered, the distance between the attributes precisely measured, and an absolute zero exists.
13. Measurement validity that relies on some independent, outside verification.
14. Measurement validity that relies upon a pre-existing and already accepted measure to verify the indicator of a construct.
15. Measurement validity that relies on the occurrence of a future event or behavior that is logically consistent to verify the indicator of a construct.
16. Measurement validity that requires that a measure represent all the aspects of the conceptual definition of a construct.
17. The definition of a variable in terms of the specific activities to measure or indicate it in the empirical world.
18. A level of measurement that identifies a difference among categories of a variable and allows the categories to be rank ordered as well.
19. A level of measurement that identifies differences among variable attributes, ranks categories, and measures distance between categories, but there is no true zero.
20. A term that means truth. It can be applied to the logical tightness of experimental design, the ability to generalize findings outside a study, the quality of measurement or the proper use of procedures.
21. A careful, systematic definition of a construct that is explicitly written to clarify one's thinking. It is often linked to other concepts or theoretical statements.
22. Variables measured on a continuum in which an infinite number of finer gradations between variable attributes are possible.
23. Variables in which the attributes can be measured only with a limited number of distinct, separate categories.
24. The ability of experimenters to strengthen a causal explanation's logical rigor by eliminating potential alternative explanations for an association between the treatment and dependent variable through an experimental design.
25. The ability to generalize from experimental research to settings or people that differ from the specific conditions of the study.
26. Many procedures or instruments that indicate, or provide evidence of, the presence or level of a variable in empirical reality. Researchers use the combination of several together to measure a variable.
27. A scale often used in survey research in which people express attitudes or other responses in terms of several ordinal-level categories (e.g., agree, disagree) that are ranked along a continuum.
28. The summing or combining of many separate measures of a construct or variable.

29. A scale that indirectly measures feelings. A researcher presents people with a topic or object and a list of many polar opposite adjectives or adverbs. People then indicate their feelings by marking one of several spaces between the two adjectives or adverbs.
30. The principle that response categories in a scale or other measure should be organized so that a person's responses fit into only one category, i.e., categories should not overlap.
31. The principle that response categories in a scale or other measure should provide a category for all possible responses, i.e., every possible response fits into some category.
32. A scale that measures the distance between two or more social groups by having members of one group express the point at which they feel comfortable with various types of social interaction or closeness with members of the other group(s).
33. A scale that researchers use after data are collected to reveal whether a hierarchical pattern exists among responses, such that people who give responses at a "higher level" also tend to give "lower level" ones.
34. A type of quantitative data measure, often used in survey research, that captures the intensity, direction, level or potency of a variable construct along a continuum. Most are at the ordinal-level of measurement.

Name _____

MATCHING KEY TERMS FOR CHAPTER 5

	Bogardus Social Distance Scale		Levels of Measurement
	Conceptual Definition		Likert Scale
	Conceptual Hypothesis		Measurement Validity
	Conceptualization		Multiple Indicators
	Concurrent Validity		Mutually Exclusive Attributes
	Content Validity		Nominal-Level Measurement
	Continuous Variables		Operational Definition
	Criterion Validity		Operationalization
	Discrete Variables		Ordinal-Level Measurement
	Empirical Hypothesis		Predictive Validity
	Exhaustive Attributes		Ratio-Level Measurement
	External Validity		Reliability
	Face Validity		Scale
	Guttman Scale		Semantic Differential
	Index		Standardization
	Internal Validity		Unidimensionality
	Interval-Level Measurement		Validity

Name _____

Exercise 5.1

Professor Milktoast conducted a study on 150 computer science students in 3 sections of Beginning Programming. He wanted to improve student learning and test a learning theory he picked up from Hank Hardnose's Dog Obedience School. He thought that dogs and students learn the most when they are highly motivated and that threats lead to greater motivation for students or dogs. He gave a speech in Section 1 on the first class day in a stern, serious tone. He emphasized that this was a very hard course. He said students would fail unless they got at least 80 percent correct on a difficult comprehensive final exam. In Section 2 he omitted the statement about the course difficulty. He used a less stern tone and said the cutoff for F's was 60 percent. In Section 3 he smiled and said this was an easy course. He stated that students only needed to get 30 percent on the final examination to pass the course. He measured motivation as the number of hours per week a student spent working on computers. He assumed that high motivation was indicated by spending at least 8 hours per week on computers. He measured learning with the final exam score. He hoped to find that Section 1 students were more likely to spend at least 8 hours a week on the computer. In addition, he to find that the students who spent at least 8 hours per week on the computer were more likely to get a higher score higher on the final examination than those who spent less than 8 hours per week.

1. What is the independent variable in general conceptual terms?

   The intervening variable?

   The dependent variable?

2. State the conceptual hypothesis of this study:

3. What is the operational definition of the independent variable?

   The intervening variable?

   The dependent variable?

4. State the empirical hypothesis of this study:

Name _____

Exercise 5.2

We know that during U.S. Presidential campaigns not everyone votes. Some people not only vote, but they are very active and talk to their friends, family, and neighbors about the party or candidate they support. Some also contribute money. Let us see whether Americans who did not did not vote, talk about the campaign, or make donations in the election fits a Guttman Scale by calculating its Coefficient of Reproducibility. If the data yields a coefficient of over .90 it is considered "Guttman Scalable."

Data are from National Election Survey, 2004

Number of People	Voted	Talked	Contributed	
37	Yes	Yes	Yes	
178	Yes	Yes	No	Pattern is
213	Yes	No	No	Scalable
76	No	No	No	
13	Yes	No	Yes	
0	No	No	Yes	"Errors"
19	No	Yes	No	
1	No	Yes	Yes	

Coefficient of Reproducibility = 1 – [Total Errors / Total Responses]

Total Errors = [All Responses – Scalable Responses]

All Responses = All people x Number of Items Answered

The Coefficient of Reproducibility = _____ .

Is the data Guttman scalable?   YES   NO

Student Workbook for Neuman, *Basics of Social Research*, 2e   45

Name _____

Exercise 5.3

First read the following newspaper article

MUDTOWN NEWS

City Officials and social service agency officials state they are concerned about this serious problem. The mayor announced the creation of a Pregnancy Task Force to investigate the problem at East High School. Principal John Jones of North High School stated that he is concerned, but feels the problem is under control. He said, "The problem at North has not reached the epidemic situation with which East High School is plagued." He will continue to monitor the problem. Sister Sue of St. Ruth's stated, "The few pregnancies at our school demonstrates the importance of a religious-based education to instill a strong moral character." Sergeant John of Sergeant John's Academy said, "I would not expect a problem at our Academy. Our students have self-discipline. Our excellent record is due to our program of rigorous academic and physical training and high standards for all students

---

After reading this article, you obtain the following enrollment statistics for each high school.

	East	North	St. Ruths	Sergeant John's
Boys	800	300	300	600
Girls	1200	600	200	8
Total	2000	900	500	608

With the enrollment statistics above, What can you say about this "news story?"

How does standardization of the data help you to understand what is occurring among students in the schools?

Name _____

Exercise 5.4

This exercise uses the CD that comes with the workbook. Go to Chapter 5. Read about Levels of Measurement on one of the first three web sites of those listed below (also listed on the CD with the workbook), then go to one of the two quiz web sites and take a quiz. Print your answers.

Levels of Measurement Lecture from CORNELL UNIVERSITY
http://www.socialresearchmethods.net/kb/measlevl.htm

Levels of Measurement Lecture from ARIZONA STATE UNIVERSITY
http://glass.ed.asu.edu/stats/lesson5/measure.htm

Levels of Measurement Quiz from CALIFORNIA STATE UNIVERSITY SAN MARCOS
http://courses.csusm.edu/soc201kb/level_of_measurement.htm

Levels of Measurement is Revision Questions 1 from CHARLES STUART UNIVERSITY (AUSTRALIA) http://life.csu.edu.au/wrobinson/measlevelsc.htm

Student Workbook for Neuman, *Basics of Social Research*, 2e   47

Name _____

Exercise 5.5

I created a five item Traditional White Racism toward Blacks Index by re-coding six questions from a U.S. national survey conducted in 2004 called the General Social Survey. You can go to the RaceEthnic data file in the CD with this workbook for the data and index.

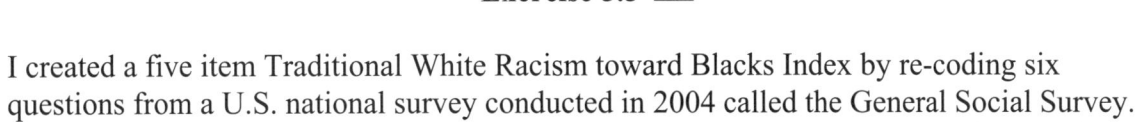

Short Variable Name	General Social Survey Question Item	NON-RACIST Code = 0	RACIST Code = 1
GOV BLACK	How do you feel about the government helping Blacks, on a scale of 1 to 5, 1 = the government is obligated to help blacks, 5 = the government should not give special treatment to blacks?	Government Help or neutral, rating 1, 2, or 3	No help, rating 4 or 5
RACE DIF1	On average Blacks have worse jobs, income and housing than Whites, is this mainly due to discrimination?	Yes	No
RACE DIF2	On average Blacks have worse jobs, income and housing than Whites, is this because most Blacks have less in-born ability to learn?	No	Yes
RACE DIF4	On average Blacks have worse jobs, income and housing than Whites, is this because most blacks don't have motivation or will power to life themselves out of poverty	No	Yes
MARRY BLK	How would you respond to a close relative marrying a Black person?	Strongly Favor, Favor or Neutral	Strongly Oppose, Oppose
BLACK WORK	What are the work habits of Blacks from 1 to 7, where 1 = Hard Working 7 is Lazy.	Hard Working or Neutral 1, 2, 3, 4 or 5	Lazy 6, 7

RACIST INDEX = GOV BLACK + RACE DIF1 + RACE DIF2 + RACE DIF 4 + MARRY BLACK + BLACK WORK

The Range of the INDEX is 0 (least racist) to 6 (most racist).
Among Whites ONLY in the 2004 national sample, the following percentage received scores of 1-6. As you will learn in Chapter 10, this is called a frequency distribution.

Index Score	Number	Percent	
0	1	0.3%	LEAST RACIST SCORE
1	29	9.4%	
2	61	19.7%	
3	89	28.8%	
4	77	24.9%	
5	43	13.9%	
6	9	2.9%	MOST RACIST SCORE
	237	100%	

To simplify we can categorize the index scores into Low (0-2), Medium (3) or High (4 or higher). Here is how Whites with various index scores answered other questions related to race relations.

Traditional Racism Index

Score

Percentage of Whites who said:	Low	Medium	High
Would you oppose living in a neighborhood where one-half of your neighbors are Black?	5.5%	15.7%	34.9%
The government spends too much to aid Blacks	7.3%	13.0%	34.9%
Blacks are not intelligent	6.6%	9.0%	18.6%
Agree or Strongly Agree with statement; Irish, Italians Jews and other groups overcame prejudice and worked their way up. Blacks should do the same without special favors.	44.0%	78.7%	95.3%

Are the people with Low Scores (0-1) less likely to give answers that appear racist?
Are those with High Scores (4 or higher) more likely to?
Do you think the index is unidimensional? Why?
Write a short essay of whether or not you think the racism index is helpful for understanding the opinions of Whites on other racially sensitive issues.

Student Workbook for Neuman, *Basics of Social Research*, 2e				49

Name _____

Exercise 5.6

This exercise uses the CD that comes with the workbook. Open SPSS on your computer [how to install/run SPSS is discussed in the front section of this workbook].

First, review page 126 of the textbook. This exercise expands on the data presented in Box 5.3 by presenting more data and updated data.

1. In the opening screen of SPSS, click on the button that says **Open an Existing Data Source**.

2. Locate the Folder or subdirectory on the Workbook CD that says SPSS Datafiles.

3. Find the file called OLYMPICS and open it.

4. Look at the data and notice the following:

   a. The names of six variables across the top.
      Country
      Number of Gold Metals won in 2000 Olympics
      Population size (in 1000s)
      Gross Domestic Product (in $ million)
      Population in 1000s per Gold Metal won
      GDP $ million per Gold Metal won

   b. Twenty-five case or country names along the side, from top to bottom.

5. Click on the top button that says **Data** and select **Sort Cases**.

6. In the box that opens, select the variable Gold Metals in the left open window with a list of variables. Now, click on the arrow button between the right and left open windows to pull it into the right window. Select **Descending** sort order (lower center) and then click on the OK button (upper right).

7. Click on the **File** button at the top, then select **Print Preview** (Zoom In to make it larger if necessary). Look at the ranking of Gold Metal winners in the 2000 Olympics held in Sydney, Australia. You will notice that the USA is ranked at the top with 40 Gold Metals. [This is a little different from Box 5.3 because I used original data here and Box 5.3 comes from an article in the *Economist* magazine before finalized results.]

8. Print the Table.

9. Repeat steps 5 and 6 above with minor changes. First, click on the Reset button to clear your previous sorting command. Select the variable Population/Gold and Select **Ascending** sort order (lower center) and then click on OK (upper right button).

10. Repeat step 7 and print the Table.

11. Repeat step 10. Only this time substitute GDP/Gold. Print the Table.

12. You now have three tables with three different rankings. The first by total number of Gold metals (unstandardized). The other two tables are standardized by population and GDP.

13. OPTIONAL. Click on **Analyze** button along the top, select **Reports**, select **Case Summaries**. Move all the variables across from the left to the right open window. Select Options below and create a new title, such as 2000 OLYMPICS GOLD METAL WINNERS and Continue when done. Click OK to create an Output View. You can print this view for the three tables if you prefer.

14. Compare the top 10 countries on each of the three tables. Write a short essay that explains how standardizing the number of Gold Metals use a base of population size or GDP changes the relative standing of countries and informs you about Olympic competition in ways that is an improvement over unstandardized data.

Data Sources:

Data on gold metals won are from the International Olympics Committee at http://www.olympics.com

$GDP data and population data are for 2000 and are from World Bank at: http://devdata.worldbank.org/data-query/.
Except for GDP data for Cuba which are from the C.I.A. World Fact Book that can be found on the Internet at: http://www.odci.gov/cia/publications/factbook/index.html.

Student Workbook for Neuman, *Basics of Social Research*, 2e   51

Name _____

Exercise 5.7

Go to the library locate an article from one of the following scholarly journals that uses quantitative data.

- *Criminology*
- *Journal of Marriage and Family*
- *Journal of Politics*
- *Social Forces*
- *Social Problems*
- *Social Science Quarterly*
- *Sociological Inquiry*
- *Sociological Quarterly.*

Attach a photocopy of the article.

1. What is the **topic** of the article?

2. What is the main conceptual **hypothesis** being tested in the article? \

3. How is the **dependent variable** defined conceptually

4. How is the **dependent variable** measured?

5. Discuss the **reliability** of the **dependent variable.**

6. Discuss the **validity** (any type) of the **dependent variable.**

7. What is a different way to measure the same **dependent variable**?

Chapter 6

QUALITATIVE AND QUANTITATIVE SAMPLING

LEARNING OBJECTIVES

After studying Chapter 6 you will be able to do the following:
1. Distinguish between random assignment and random sampling;
2. Describe the meaning a *population*, a *population parameter*, sampling elements, and *sampling frames*;
3. Describe various types of non-probability samples and explain when each is appropriate;
4. Explain why random sampling produces more representative samples than non-random sampling and the types of sampling qualitative research uses;
5. Understand the concept of *sampling distribution* and the basic principle represented by the *Central Limit Theorem*;
6. Calculate a *sampling ratio* and a *sampling interval*;
7. Describe when a *systematic sample* or *stratified sample* is appropriate and how to carry out each;
8. Describe when a *cluster sample* is appropriate and why/when *PPS* is necessary;

KEY TERMS MATCHING DEFINITIONS, CHAPTER 6

1. A type of random sample in which a researcher creates a sampling frame and uses a pure random process to select cases, each sampling element in the population will have an equal probability of being selected.
2. A diagram or "map" that shows the network of social relationships, influence patterns or communication paths among a group of people or units.
3. A characteristic of the entire population that is estimated from a sample.
4. A type of non-random sample in which the researcher begins with one case, then based on information about relationships from that case, identifies others, and repeats the process.
5. A type of non-random sample in which the researcher first identifies general categories into which cases or people will be selected, then he or she selects cases reach a predetermined number of cases in each category.
6. A type of random sample in which the researcher first identifies a set of mutually-exclusive and exhaustive categories, then uses a random selection method to select cases for each category.
7. The name for a case or single unit to be selected into a sample.
8. The name for the large general group of many cases from which a researcher draws a sample and which is usually stated in theoretical terms.
9. The name for the large general group of many cases from which a sample is drawn and which is specified in very concrete terms.
10. A list of cases in a population, or the best approximation of it.

11. The number of cases in the sample divided by the number of cases in the population or the sampling frame, or the proportion of the population in the sample.
12. The inverse of the sampling ratio which is used in systematic sampling to select cases.
13. A method of randomly selecting cases for telephone interviews that uses all possible telephone numbers as a sampling frame.
14. A type of non-random sample in which the researcher uses a wide range of methods to locate all possible cases of a highly specific and difficult to reach population.
15. A type of non-random sample in which the researcher selects anyone.
16. A list of numbers which has no pattern in them and which is used to create a random process for selecting cases and other randomization purposes.
17. How much a sample deviates from being representative of the population.
18. A type of random sample that uses multiple stages and is often used to cover wide geographic areas in which aggregated units are randomly selected then samples are drawn from the sampled aggregated units, or clusters.
19. An adjustment made in cluster sampling when the each cluster does not have the same number of sampling elements.
20. A distribution created by drawing many random samples from the same population.
21. A law-like mathematical relationship which states: Whenever many random samples are drawn from a population and plotted a normal distribution is formed, and the center of the such a distribution for a variable is equal to its population parameter.
22. A range of values, usually a little higher and lower than a specific value found in a sample, within which a researcher has a specified and high degree of confidence that the population parameter lies.
23. A type of random sample in which a researcher selects every kth (e.g., 12th) case in the sampling frame using a sampling interval.
24. A branch of applied mathematics or statistics based on a random sample. It lets a researcher make precise statements about the level of confidence she has in the results of a sample being equal to the population parameter.
25. A numerical estimate of a population parameter computed from a sample.
26. A small set of cases selected from a larger pool that can be generalized to the population.
27. A type of non-random sample, used by qualitative researchers, in which a researcher selects unusual or non-conforming cases purposely to provide insight into social processes.
28. People who engage in clandestine, deviant or concealed activities and who are difficult to locate and study.
29. A type of sample in which the sampling elements are selected using something other than a mathematically random process.
30. A type of sample in which the researcher uses a random number table or similar mathematical random process so that each sampling element in the population will have an equal probability of being selected.
31. A type of non-random sample in which a researcher tries to find as many relevant cases as possible, until time, financial resources, or his/her energy are exhausted, or until there is no new information or diversity from the cases.

Name _____

MATCHING KEY TERMS FOR CHAPTER 6

	Central Limit Theorem		Sample
	Cluster Sampling		Sampling Distribution
	Confidence Intervals		Sampling Element
	Deviant Case Sampling		Sampling Error
	Haphazard Sampling		Sampling Frame
	Hidden Populations		Sampling Interval
	Inferential Statistics		Sampling Ratio
	Nonrandom Sample		Sequential Sampling
	Parameter		Simple Random Sampling
	Population		Snowball Sampling
	Probability Proportionate to Size [PPS]		Sociogram
	Purposive Sampling		Statistic
	Quota Sampling		Stratified Sampling
	Random Digit Dialing [RDD]		Systematic Sampling
	Random Number Table		Target Population
	Random Sample		

Student Workbook for Neuman, *Basics of Social Research*, 2e   55

Name _____

Exercise 6.1

Draw a **two-stage random sample** of 60 names from the directory of student telephone numbers of your college or university. The directory is your sampling frame. If your directory separates students from others, just use student names, if it combines students with faculty and staff use the entire list of names.

Stage 1: Draw a Simple Random Sample of Clusters (Pages)

Count the number of pages with students names in the directory. Randomly select 10 pages by using a simple random sample method. Use the CD that came with this workbook.

For *Sample* put the CD in the microcomputer (NOTE: this is only available on Windows versions). For the population enter the number of relevant pages, for the sample size enter 10. The 10 number on the screen constitute a simple random sample of the pages. Photocopy the 10 pages from the directory to use in the next stage.

Stage 2: Draw a Systematic Sample from the Clusters

Each page is a cluster with sampling elements. In order to draw a systematic sample of six names from a cluster you must first compute the sampling interval for each page. Unless your telephone directory has exactly the same number of names on each page you have to compute a separate sampling interval for each of the 10 pages.

To compute a sampling interval count the total number of names on a page and divide it by your sample size for the cluster which is 6. For example, you find 110 names on a page 110/6 = 18.3. Round to the nearest whole number, or 18 in the example. Before you begin you need a random starting point. To get this you can use the program *Sample*.

For the *Sample* program just enter the total number of names on the page as your population and 1 as your sample size.

Beginning at your random start, count down by the sampling interval. For example, with a random start of the 22nd name and sampling interval of 18, the 40th name is the first one in your sample. You would next go another 18 names to the 58th one and add it to your sample, and so forth.

Once you get to the end of the page you will not have 6 names for the sample unless your random number was smaller than your <u>sampling interval</u>. Just continue to the beginning, as if the first name on the
page came after the last one. Repeat the process for each of the 10 pages.

Turn in the 10 photocopied pages. Show your work shown on them and the computations of sampling intervals for each and the 60 names you randomly selected.

Stage 3: Estimate the <u>Sampling Ratio</u>.

You now have a <u>sample</u> of 60 student names.

To estimate the <u>sampling ratio</u> you first need to compute the approximate number of names in the <u>sampling frame</u>. Take the average number of total names on the 10 pages and multiply this number by the total number of pages in the directory (you counted this for Stage 1). Now you have the <u>sample size</u> and an estimate of the population size. Compute the <u>sampling ratio</u>.

Fill in the following

1. Sampling Frame: _____

2. Number of pages with student names: _____

3. Sampling ratio for sample of 10 pages: _____

4. Sampling Interval for each page

   Number of names on page: ___ ___ ___ ___ ___ ___ _____ ___

   Sampling Interval: ___ ___ ___ ___ ___ ___ ___ _____ ___

5. Estimated population size (number of students in directory): _____

6. Sampling ratio of the 60 sampled names: _____

Student Workbook for Neuman, *Basics of Social Research*, 2e

Name _____

Exercise 6.2

Illiteracy rates by sex, adults in 35 selected African nations (as of July 2005)

COUNTRY	Male	Female
Algeria	78.8	61
Angola	56	28
Botswana	76.9	82.4
Cameroon	84.7	73.4
Central African Republic	63.3	39.9
Chad	56	39.3
Congo, Republic of the	89.6	78.4
Cote d'Ivoire	57.9	43.6
Egypt	68.3	46.9
Ethiopia	50.3	35.1
Gabon	73.7	53.3
Ghana	82.7	67.1
Kenya	90.6	79.7
Lesotho	74.5	94.5
Liberia	73.3	41.6
Libya	92.4	72
Madagascar	75.5	62.5
Malawi	76.1	49.8
Mali	53.5	39.6
Mauritania	51.8	31.9
Morocco	64.1	39.4
Mozambique	63.5	32.7
Namibia	84.4	83.7
Nigeria	75.7	60.6
Rwanda	76.3	64.7
Senegal	50	30.7
South Africa	87	85.7
Sudan	71.8	50.5
Tanzania	85.9	70.7
Togo	75.4	46.9
Tunisia	84	64.4
Uganda	79.5	60.4
Zambia	86.8	74.8
Zimbabwe	94.2	87.2

INSTRUCTIONS

1. Take the first 10 nations (haphazard sample) and compute average illiteracy rates for males and for women (you will have two samples, one sample for male and one for females).

2. Take every fifth nation (a systematic sample with a sampling interval of 5, beginning with Kenya). Compute the male and female illiteracy rates averages for 7 nations. Treat the list as a circle, so if you reach the end continue at the beginning.

3. Draw simple random samples of 10 nations (see Exercise 8.1 on how). Compute the average illiteracy rates for the 10 in your sample. Compute the average illiteracy rates for males and for women.

4. Compute the averages of the same male and female illiteracy rates for the population, or all 35 nations on the list.

5. Do your haphazard, systematic, and simple random samples (#1, 2, 3) for males and female differ from the population parameters? Discuss what you found.

Data Sources: [from Nationmaster.com]

Student Workbook for Neuman, *Basics of Social Research*, 2e   59

Name _____

Exercise 6.3

SNOWBALL SAMPLE: Locate 4 students who you have never seen with one another. Ask each in **Round 1** to name two other students attending the same college with whom they are friends.

For **Round 2** locate each of the friends and repeat (we can call these two friends A and B), only ask them not to name the first student who gave their name. For **Round 3** go to each of these students (A and B) and repeat, asking each to name two students who are friends. It has to be someone other than Round 2, but it could be any student named in Round 1. You will get 8 student names in round one, 16 in round two and 36 in round three, or 56 in total.

1. Draw a sociogram of your snowball sample

2. How many students in round three were present in Round 1?

ROUND 1	*Student naming friends*			
	Student 1	Student 2	Student 3	Student 4
Person named				
Close Friend 1	1.	2.	3.	4.
Close Friend 2	5.	6.	7.	8.

ROUND 2	*Student naming friends*			
	Student 1's Friend 1	Student 2's Friend 1	Student 3's Friend 1	Student 4's Friend 1
Person named				
Friend A	9.	10.	11.	12.
Friend B	13.	14.	15.	16.
	Student 1's Friend 2	Student 2's Friend 2	Student 3's Friend 2	Student 4's Friend 2
Person named				
Friend A	17.	18.	19.	20.
Friend B	21.	22.	23.	24.

ROUND 3   *Student naming friends*

	1 F1, A	2 F1 A	3 F1, A	4 F1, A
Person named				
Friend X	25.	26.	27.	28.
Friend Y	29.	30.	31.	32.

	1 F1, B	2 F1 B	3 F1, B	4 F1, B
Person named				
Friend X	33.	34.	35.	36.
Friend Y	37.	38.	39.	40.

	1 F2, A	2 F2 A	3 F2, A	4 F2, A
Person named				
Friend X	41.	42.	43.	44.
Friend Y	45.	46.	47.	48.

	1 F2, B	2 F2 B	3 F2, B	4 F2, B
Person named				
Friend X	49.	50.	51.	52.
Friend Y	53.	54.	55.	56.

Name _____

Exercise 6.4

QUOTA SAMPLE:

Select two characteristics for quota groups (common ones are sex, age, race, year or class in college, general type of major). Cross classify the two characteristics to create four to six categories. For example,

Age Group		
Under 20		
20–22		
23 or higher		

Put a number in each category of the table for a total of 30 students. For example, 5 in each of the categories above would be 5 males under 20, 5 females under 20, 5 males 20-22 years old, etc.

Now go to a location with many students. Approach students one at a time and tell them that you are doing a quick survey and have to ask their age and major. Record the age, sex and major of each student you contact. Once you have "filled your quota" try to avoid asking people who look the same (e.g., if you need 5 females over 23 and have all 5, do not approach any more females who appear to be over 23). You may have to go to more than one location more than one time to "fill you quota." Stop asking once you have the number of people in each category you pre-set.

1. How many students in total did you have to contact in order to fill your quota?

2. Which category did you approach the most people, more than needed for your quota, in trying to get your quota filled?

3. Which category, if any, did you contact exactly the number needed to fill the quota and no more.

Name _____

PRACTICE QUIZ 3, CHAPTERS 5–6 (17 questions)

1. If you went to a restaurant and saw the following lists of dessert choices which is **both mutually exclusive and exhaustive**?

<u>A</u>	<u>B</u>	<u>C</u>	<u>D</u>	<u>E</u>
Apples	Jello	Brownies	Rice Pudding	Apple Pie
Fruit	Bananas	Cookies	Ice Cream	Oatmeal Cookies
Cake	Ice Cream	Baked Sweets	Pie	Cherry Pie
Ice Cream	Grapes	Fruit	Fruit	Chocolate Brownies
Other	Pineapple	Other	Other	Cheese Cake

2. The variable educational level was measured as degree or certificate in school completed (not high school, high school, vocational/technical or two year, four-year college, graduate degree). It is, therefore, measured at the ____ level.

   a. nominal
   b. interval
   c. ratio
   d. ordinal
   e. not enough information to decide

3. What is the difference between Validity and Reliability when measuring variables?
   a. Nothing, they are two words for the same thing.
   b. Validity refers to how consistent results of a measure are, while reliability refers to whether or not the measure really measures what it is supposed to measure.
   c. Reliability refers to how consistent results of a measure are, while validity refers to whether or not the measure really measures what it is supposed to measure.
   d. Reliability refers to a situation when the researcher uses a random sample, Validity to a situation when the researcher has a census or the entire population.
   e. Validity is used for unbiased samples, reliability for biased samples.

Use for 4 and 5

Hicks and Misra (1993, *American Journal of Sociology* 99:668-710) tested whether the "welfare effort in affluent postwar democracies" can be accounted for by the "use of government authority by the left" and "use of disruption by the working class." The authors tested the theory by looking at data on 18 large democracies for the years 1960-1982. They measured welfare effort as the "share of the gross national product" for welfare (e.g. education, social security, aid to the poor). They measured leftist power by the percent of cabinet positions held by left-wing political parties. For a measure of working class disruption, they used the number of "man-days" loss due to strikes and work stoppages. Their data for the share of the gross national product came from the International Labor Organization, data for leftist power and strikes came from previous studies by other researchers.

4. In this study, the **operational definition** of the **dependent variable** is:

    a. man-hours loss due to strikes and work stoppages
    b. welfare effort
    c. share of a nation's gross national product spent on welfare
    d. International Labor Organization
    e. use of government authority by the left

5. In this study, the **operational definition** one of the two **independent variables** is:

    a. the nation
    b. the strike or work stoppage
    c. the individual
    d. the welfare program
    e. the organization supplying data (e.g. International Labor Organization)

6. Dr. Ladysmith wants to develop an ordinal measure of prejudice toward and avoidance of people who are HIV-positive. What measurement technique should she consider given her situation?

    a. Bogardus Social Distance Scale
    b. Likert Scale
    c. Semantic Differential
    d. Index
    e. Guttman Scale

7. You find the following number of armed robberies in four cities and their population size for 2002:

Armed	Robberies	Population Size
City A	100	200,000 people
City B	150	300,000 people
City C	300	600,000 people
City D	500	1 million people

Which city had the highest crime rate for armed robberies in 2001?

a. City A
b. City B
c. City C
d. City D
e. All have the same rate

Use for 8 to 10

The Citizens Utility Board (CUB) is opposing a request for a rate hike by several utility companies. The utilities say rates have to be increased to guarantee their shareholders a 16 percent rate of return. CUB argues that utility companies are monopolies delivering a necessity, so the rate hike is too high, especially for the poor. CUB decides to get additional information for an upcoming Public Service Commission hearing and contracts with you to find out how much households spend on necessities. You are to check the amount spent last year on food (excluding meals eaten away from home), utilities (electricity and gas), and rent or house payments. CUB provided you with a list of all 1 million gas and electric residential customers from the utility companies. To draw the sample you took every 500th address on the list and recorded the total amount of last year's utility bill. Next, you asked the person calling him/herself the "head of the household" how much the household spent on groceries and rent or house payments.

8. In this study each address of a residential customer is your:

a. Sampling frame
b. Population unit
c. Sampling interval
d. Sampling unit
e. Sampling element

9. How large is your sample?

   a. 200
   b. 500
   c. 2,000
   d. 2,500
   e. 5,000

10. What type of sampling was used?

    a. Cluster
    b. PPS
    c. RDD
    d. Stratified
    e. Systematic

11. Sally draws a sample to survey the students at Friendlyville Middle School. The school records show that there are 1,000 students enrolled in the school. Sally's sample has 150 students. What is her **SAMPLING RATIO**?

    a. .015
    b. 0.15
    c. 15
    d. 150
    e. Insufficient information given to calculate

12. I want to draw a sample of the employees at a large hospital and be certain that my sample contains people from all personnel categories: physicians, nurses, administrators, cleaning staff, technicians, etc. I want to use a kind of probability sample. Which type of sample is best, i.e., lowest sampling error?

    a. Simple random sampling
    b. Quota sampling
    c. Cluster sampling
    d. Stratified sampling
    e. Accidental sampling

13. Which of the following is NOT a condition that suggests you should be using Probability Proportionate to Size Sampling (PPS)?

    a. Cluster sampling is used
    b. Units (states, blocks, etc.) are of unequal size
    c. Snowball sampling is used
    d. a and c
    e. a and b

14. Which of the following is TRUE about Sample Size

a. There is a simple rule: the biggest sample is always better.
b. Increases in sample size are subject to diminishing returns
c. In general, you need to take about 10 percent of the population to get a good sample size
d. You need a bigger sample size if your population is homogeneous (similar)
e. You don't need as large of a sample, if what you are interested in studying in a very rare or unusual characteristic in the population

Figure 1: The Measurement Process

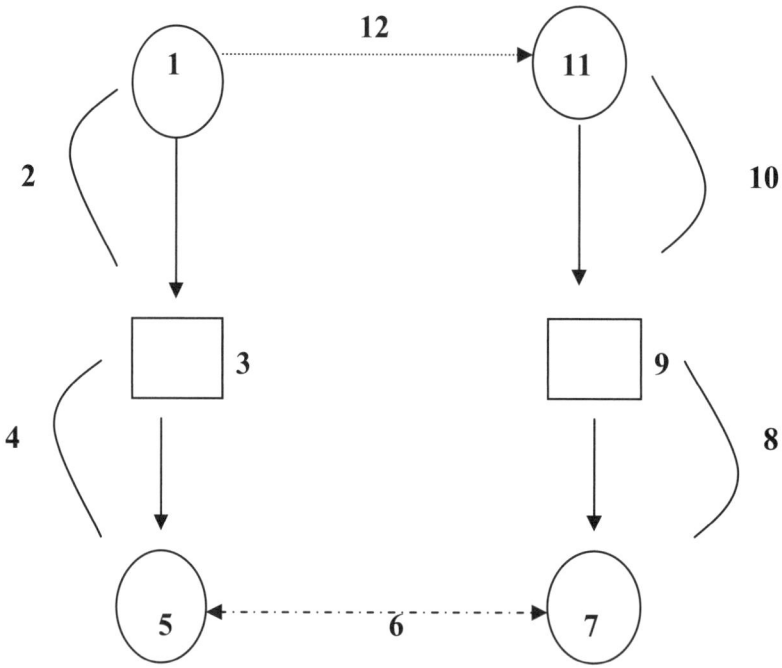

Use the following to answer choices for questions 15-17

a. Operational definition of the Dependent Variable
b. Conceptual definition of the Dependent Variable
c. Operational definition of the Independent Variable
d. Conceptual definition of the Independent Variable
e. The Concept/Construct of Independent Variable

15. What does #9 symbolize?
16. What does #1 symbolize?
17. What does #5 symbolize?

CHAPTER 7

SURVEY RESEARCH

LEARNING OBJECTIVES

After studying Chapter 7 you will be able to do the following:
1. Recognize errors in survey question writing and write survey questions that avoid the errors;
2. Understand the issues involved with asking threatening questions in survey research;
3. Know the purpose of a contingency question and how to use it appropriately;
4. Describe advantages and disadvantages of open versus closed-ended survey questions;
5. Explain the purpose and use of filter and quasi-filter survey questions;
6. Understand questionnaire design issues such as question order, layout, and questionnaire length;
7. Explain advantages and disadvantages of mail, telephone interview, and face-to-face interview surveys;
8. Understand the differences between a survey research interview and an ordinary conversation.

KEY TERM MATCHING DEFINITIONS, CHAPTER 7

1. A problem in survey research question writing that occurs when a highly respected group or individual is linked to one of the answers.
2. The name of a survey research questionnaire when a telephone or face-to-face interview is used.
3. A survey question that has more than one idea and is stated in a confusing way that makes it unclear whether each idea separately is being asked or only the combination of both together.
4. A follow-up question or action in survey research used by an interviewer to have a respondent clarify or elaborate on an incomplete or inappropriate answer.
5. A type of survey research question in which respondents must choose from a fixed set of answers.
6. A type of survey research question in which respondents are free to offer any answer they wish to the question.
7. A type of survey research question in which respondents are given a fixed set of answers to choose from, but in addition an "other" category is offered so that they can specify a different answer.
8. A bias in survey research in which respondents are give a "normative" response or a socially acceptable answer rather than give a truthful answer.
9. A type of survey research question in which respondents are likely to cover up or lie about their true behavior or beliefs because they fear a loss of self-image or that they may appear to be undesirable or deviant.

10. Respondents who lack a belief or opinion, but who give an answer anyway if asked in a <u>survey research</u> question, often their answers are inconsistent.
11. An effect that occurs when a specific term or word used in a <u>survey research</u> question affects how respondents answer the question.
12. An effect in <u>survey research</u> when respondents tend to agree with every question in a series rather than thinking through their answer to each question.
13. An effect in <u>survey research</u> in which respondents hear some specific questions before others, and the earlier questions affect their answers to later questions.
14. An effect <u>survey research</u> when an overall tone or set topics heard by a respondent affects how they interpret the meaning of subsequent questions.
15. A way to order <u>survey research</u> questions in a <u>questionnaire</u> from general ones to specific.
16. One or more pages at the beginning of a <u>questionnaire</u> with information about an interview or respondent.
17. A type of <u>survey research</u> question in which a set of questions are listed in a compact form together and all the questions share the same set of answer categories.
18. A type of <u>survey research</u> question that includes the answer choice of "no opinion" or "don't know."
19. A type of <u>survey research</u> question in which respondents are first asked whether they have an opinion or know about a topic, then only the respondents with an opinion or knowledge are asked a specific question on the topic.
20. <u>Survey research</u> in which interviewer sits before a computer screen and keyboard, reads from the screen questions to be asked in a telephone interview, then enters answers directly into the computer.
21. A type of survey research question, based on the answer to the question a respondent next goes to one or another later question.
22. A type of survey research question in which the answer categories fail to include a choice of 'no opinion' or 'don't know.'

Name _____

MATCHING KEY TERMS FOR CHAPTER 7

	Closed-Ended Question		Open-ended Question
	Computer Assisted Telephone Interviewing CATI		Order Effects
	Context Effects		Partially-Open Question
	Contingency Question		Prestige Bias
	Cover sheet		Probe
	Double-barreled Question		Quasi-Filter Question
	Floaters		Response Set
	Full-Filter Question		Social Desirability Bias
	Funnel Sequence		Standard-Format Question
	Interview Schedule		Threatening Questions
	Matrix Question		Wording Effects

Name _____

Exercise 7.1

1. Write a hypothesis with two variables that is appropriate for survey research about a non-sensitive issue appropriate for college students. Write two questions to measure each variable (four in total). Indicate whether each question is measuring an attitude, behavior, etc. Indicate whether the variable is measured at the nominal, ordinal, interval or ratio level.

2. Design and type a 15 item questionnaire for a face-to-face interview from beginning to end including the four questions from number 1. Include instructions to interviewers and respondents, order the questions appropriately, etc. Include at least one of each of the following. Also, identify the question for each by writing the type of question in parenthesis next to it.
   - a contingency question
   - a full filter question
   - a quasi-filter question
   - a partially open question
   - an open question
   - a closed question

3. Locate two college students who are strangers. Ask them for their permission. Now tape record an interview each person separately. After you are done, ask if they understood all questions or found any confusing. Listen to the tape recording afterward. Note whether any of the following occurred:
   - a question not read exactly,
   - an incorrect probe
   - potentially biasing question
   - unclear answer

4. Turn in the following:
   (a) answer to #1, (b) questionnaire, (c) tape recording, (d) answer to #3.

Name _____

Exercise 7.2

Use the CD that comes with the workbook for this exercise and connect to the Internet. Follow the instructions in the workbook preface. From the table of contents, go to Chapter 7.

Under Polls and Survey Data go to **Public Agenda** by clicking on it. Once at the Public Agenda web site, do the following:

- Select one public issue (lower left side)
- Read the information about it and Fact File "Understanding the Issue"
- Go to Public Opinion section and clink on the highlighted questions.
- Look at the poll results and the following details about the poll (click on **FOR MORE DETAILS**:

    1) The wording of the survey question asked
    2) The date of the survey
    3) The sponsor of the survey
    4) How the survey was conducted (e.g., telephone, mail, etc.).
    5) Number of Respondents

EXAMPLE:
Issue: Immigration
Results: Over one-half of Americans say immigration contributes more to the United States (51%) than say it causes problems (31%).

1) Question: Overall, would you say most recent immigrants to the United States contribute to this country, or do most of them cause problems?
2) November 10-13, 2001
3) Survey Organization: CBS News and The New York Times
4) Telephone interview
5) 1,995 adults

Now write up a two-page essay explaining the issue, the poll results and how the survey was conducted with exact wording to get the poll results.

Name _____

Exercise 7.3

Use the CD that comes with the workbook for this exercise and connect to the Internet. Follow the instructions in the workbook preface. From the table of contents, go to Chapter 7 page.

Under Polls and Survey Data go to **Roper Poll** by clicking on it. First on the left side, click on About the Center and read about the Roper Center. Go Back or click Home to return to the first page.

Now click Go to the Public Opinion Matters (Left side bar) then pick a topic, then pick a survey question., click VIEW to get details.

1. The wording of the survey question asked
2. The date of the survey
3. The sponsor of the survey
4. Number of Respondents
5. How the survey was conducted (e.g., telephone, mail, etc.).

EXAMPLE: Issue Abortion
Specific Issue: Do you consider yourself pro-life or pro-choice?
1. On the issue of abortion, would you say you are more pro-life or more pro-choice?
2. February 28–March 1, 2006
3. Fox News
4. 900 registered voters from a national sample
5. Telephone interviews

Do this for two survey questions and write up a two-page essay explaining the issue, the poll results and how the survey was conducted with exact wording to get the poll results.
Before you leave the Roper Poll site click on their LINKS and explore other survey research sites on the Internet.

Name _____

Exercise 7.4

Use the CD that comes with the workbook for this exercise and connect to the Internet. Follow the instructions in the workbook preface. From the table of contents, go to the Chapter 7 page.
Under Polls and Survey Data go to **Gallup** by clicking on it. Note: Gallup information is limited to subscribers but you can get a free 30 day trail subscription by signing up on-line.

- Click on Poll Topics A to Z (Left sidebar)
- Pick a topic
- Select three survey questions that were asked in the poll and do the following

1) Give the exact wording of the survey question and evaluate how well it was written, whether there were any problems with it.
2) Discuss the results that were found in the data.
3) Discuss how the survey questions were asked, the specific methodology (sample size, etc.)

Exercise 7.5

Use the CD that comes with the workbook for this exercise and connect to the Internet. Follow the instructions in the workbook preface. From the table of contents, go to the Chapter 7 page.
Under Polls and Survey Data go to Pew Research Center http://people-press.org/ by clicking on it. Once at the **Pew Research Center** site, do the following:

- Look at Featured Survey and other survey
- Read the About This Survey and Questionnaire links at the bottom of the page on the left.
- Click on the About Methodology link at the very bottom of most pages on the right side and read what it says.

Discuss the results that were found in the data. Discuss how the survey questions were asked, the specific methodology, and main findings.

Chapter 8

EXPERIMENTAL RESEARCH

LEARNING OBJECTIVES

After studying Chapter 8 you will be able to do the following:
1. Recognize the research questions and situations for which experimental research is most appropriate;
2. Describe *random assignment* and know how to randomly assign;
3. Discuss the parts of an experiment and the steps needed to conduct one;
4. Read design notation, recognize the *design notation* of major experimental designs, and translate a verbal description of an experiment into *design notation* symbols;
5. Describe *factorial designs* in a shorthand way and explain main and *interaction effects*;
6. Explain threats to *internal validity*;
7. Explain *external validity* and compare *laboratory* with *field experiments*;
8. Discuss the problem of *reactivity* and how it relates to the use of *double blind experiments*;
9. Examine the results of an experimental design and make comparisons to recognize whether major threats to *internal validity* are present;
10. Explain why researchers use *deception* in experiments and the obligations that come with a researcher using it.

KEY TERMS MATCHING DEFINITIONS, CHAPTER 8

1. A false treatment or one that has no effect in an experiment. It is sometimes called a "sugar pill" that a subject mistakes for a true treatment.
2. The name for people who are studied and participate in experimental research.
3. A threat to internal validity when groups in an experiment are not equivalent at the beginning of the experiment.
4. What the independent variable in experimental research is called.
5. When a researcher gives a true explanation of the experiment to subjects after using deception.
6. A type of experimental design that considers the impact of several independent variables simultaneously.
7. Threats to internal validity due to subjects failing to participate through the entire experiment.
8. The group that receives the treatment in experimental research.
9. Dividing subjects into groups at the beginning of experimental research using a random process, so the experimenter can treat the groups as equivalent.
10. An experimental design in which the dependent variable is measured periodically across many time points, and the treatment occurs in the midst of such measures, often only once.
11. When an experimenter lies to subjects about the true nature of an experiment or creates a false impression through his/her actions or the setting.
12. A threat to internal validity that occurs when the treatment "spills over" from the

experimental group and control group subjects modify their behavior because they learn of the treatment.
13. An experimental design used to examine whether the order or sequence in which subjects receive multiple versions of the treatment has an effect.
14. The measurement of the dependent variable of an experiment prior to the treatment.
15. The measurement of the dependent variable in experimental research after the treatment.
16. An effect of reactivity named after a famous case in which subjects reacted to the fact that they were in an experiment more than they reacted to the treatment.
17. A threat to internal validity in experimental research due to natural processes of growth, boredom, etc. which occur to subjects during the experiment and affect the dependent variable.
18. An experimental design that has random assignment, a control group, an experimental group, and pretests and posttests for each group.
19. An experimental design with only an experimental group and a posttest, no pretest.
20. A threat to internal validity due to something that occurs and affects the dependent variable during an experiment, but which is unplanned and outside the control of the experimenter.
21. The name of a symbol system used to show parts of an experiment and to make diagrams of them.
22. An experimental design in which subjects are randomly assigned to two control groups and two experimental groups. Only one experimental group and one control group receive a pretest. All four groups receive a posttest.
23. A type of experimental research in which neither the subjects nor the person who directly deals with the subjects for the experimenter knows the specifics of the experiment.
24. Experimental research that takes place in a natural setting.
25. Experimental research in an artificial setting over which the experimenter has great control.
26. The group that receives the treatment in an experiment.
27. An experimental design in which there are several repeated pretests, posttests, and treatments for one group often over a period of time.
28. An experimental design with two groups, no random assignment, and only a posttest.
29. The general threat to external validity that arises because subjects are aware that they are in an experiment and being studied.
30. Experimental designs that lack random assignment or use short-cuts and are much weaker than the classical experimental design. They are be substituted in situations where an experimenter cannot use all the features of a classical experimental design, but have weaker internal validity.
31. Experimental designs that are stronger than pre-experimental designs. They are variations on the classical experimental design and are used in special situations or when an experimenter has limited control over the independent variable.
32. The group that does not get the treatment in experimental research.
33. The effect of two independent variable that operate simultaneously together. The effect of the variables together is greater than what would occur from a simple addition of the effects from each. The variables operate together on one another to create an extra "boost."

Name _____

MATCHING KEY TERMS FOR CHAPTER 8

	Control Group		Maturation
	Classical Experimental Design		Latin Square Design
	Debrief		Mortality
	Deception		One Shot Case Study
	Design Notation		Placebo
	Diffusion of Treatment		Posttest
	Double Blind Experiment		Pre-experimental Designs
	Equivalent Time Series		Pretest
	Experimental Design		Quasi-Experimental Designs
	Experimental Group		Random Assignment
	Factorial Design		Reactivity
	Field Experiment		Selection Bias
	Hawthorne Effect		Solomon Four Group Design
	History Effects		Static Group Comparison
	Interaction Effects		Subjects
	Interrupted Time Series Design		Treatment
	Laboratory Experiment		

Name _____

Exercise 8.1

In October, 2005 the president of Big Cheese Corp. told the market research department he wanted to increase the sales of its imitation, processed whipped "cheese food" called WHIPPO. It had artificial coloring and artificial flavoring and eighteen preservatives. The research staff examined total sales (in dollars) for the months of November and December. They pulled all the existing containers of WHIPPO off the shelf on January 1, 2006 and replaced them with the same product with a new a label. It said "TASTES JUST LIKE THE OLD FASHIONED SPREAD GRANDMOTHER MADE." The label had a drawing of a woman dressed in 19th century clothing. They computed how many dollars in sales WHIPPO had for January, February and March. On April 1, 2006 they pulled in all the "Grandmother" labeled containers. They replaced the label on the containers with one which said, "NEW AND IMPROVED FOR QUICK ENERGY AND NUTRITIONAL BALANCE." It had a photo of an attractive, scantly clad young woman riding a bicycle built for two with a bare-chested muscular young man. They then checked on how many dollars in sales WHIPPO had for April, May and June.

1. Draw the experiment symbolically using **DESIGN NOTATION**? What is the name for this type of design?

2. What is the **INDEPENDENT VARIABLE** in the study?

3. What is the **DEPENDENT VARIABLE** in the study?

4. What are the **UNITS OF ANALYSIS** in the study?

Name _____

Exercise 8.2

Dr. Wacko wanted to see whether heavy doses of sex, drugs, or rock and roll improved student self-esteem more than traditional methods of counseling or no treatment at all over a six week period. He randomly assigned four groups of 30 students to two groups. In all four groups the control group received no special treatment.

- In Experimental Group A he gave the students favorable information about illegal drug use, supplied them with quantities of several types of illegal drugs free of charge, and encouraged them to try the drugs.
- In Experimental Group B he told the students about the history of rock and roll and gave them portable stereo players with a large quantity of rock and roll music. He also encouraged them to listen to the music at least six hours per day.
- In Experimental Group C he told the students the benefits of premarital sex and encouraged them to experiment with sexual behavior. He introduced them to attractive members of the opposite sex who had very liberal sexual attitudes. He also supplied them with contraceptives and private rooms.
- In Experimental Group D he placed the students in traditional counseling to improve self-esteem.

NOTE: He measured Self-Esteem with a questionnaire in which self-esteem went from 0 = very negative to 100 = very positive.

Self Esteem Score and (Number of Students)

		Pretest	Posttest
A.	**Experimental**	**65 (15)**	**63 (13)**
	Control	60 (15)	66 (14)
B.	**Experimental**	**65 (15)**	**89 (14)**
	Control	45 (15)	79 (14)
C.	**Experimental**	**66 (15)**	**90 (6)**
	Control	65 (15)	67 (14)
D	**Experimental**	**64 (15)**	**88 (14)**
	Control	63 (15)	66 (15)

1. Which set suggests that *experimental mortality* is an issue? Why?

2. Which set suggests that *internal validity* is not a noticeable problem and the independent variable had an effect? Why?

3. Which set suggests that *selection bias* is a problem? Why?

4. What happened in the set leftover after you answered 1, 2 and 3?

Name _____

Exercise 8.3

Locate two of the following four experimental research articles.

- Barreto, Manuela and Naomi Ellemers. 2005. "The Perils of Political Correctness: Men's and Women's Response to Old-Fashioned and Modern Sexist Views." *Social Psychology Quarterly* 68:75-87.

- Ong, A. and C. Ward. 1999. "The Effects of Sex and Power Schemes, Attitudes Toward Women and Victim Resistance on Rape Attributions" *Journal of Applied Social Psychology* 29:362-376.

- Kemmelmeier, Markus. 2005. "The Effects of Race and Social Dominance Orientation in Simulated Juror Decision Making." *Journal of Applied Social Psychology*; 35:1030-1045.

- Rind, B. and D. Strohmetz. 1999. "Effect on Restaurant Ripping of a Helpful Message Written on the Back of Customer's Checks" *Journal of Applied Social Psychology* 29:139-144.

Answer the following about the two articles:

1. Describe the subjects. How many groups were there? How were subjects assigned to groups?

2. What is the experimental design in design notation symbols?

3. What hypothesis (or hypotheses) was tested?

4. What was the treatment or independent variable? How was it introduced?

5. What was the dependent variable? How was it measured?

6. What possible problems with internal validity do you see in the experiment?

Name _____

Exercise 8.4

Select a report of an experiment published in a scholarly journal since 2000. Good journals to check are *Social Psychology Quarterly, Journal of Applied Social Psychology, or Journal of Experimental Social Psychology*. Attach a photocopy of the article. Write three page summary of the article in which you address all of the following nine questions.

1. Describe the subjects. How many groups were there? How were subjects assigned to groups?

2. What is the experimental design in design notation symbols?

3. What hypothesis (or hypotheses) was tested?

4. Was it a laboratory or field experiment?

5. What was the treatment or independent variable? How was it introduced?

6. What was the dependent variable? How was it measured?

7. Were there any "manipulation checks" used to evaluate the measures of variables?

8. What possible problems with internal validity do you see in the experiment?

9. What external validity problems do you see in the experiment?

Student Workbook for Neuman, *Basics of Social Research*, 2e   81

Name _____

Exercise 8.5

DESIGN AN EXPERIMENT: [Read all of the instructions first.]

1. Select a topic appropriate for an experiment and narrow down the topic to a research problem or question appropriate for an experiment. Phrase it as a question.

2. Identify 1-2 specific conceptual hypotheses that are linked to the research question in #1.

3. Identify the independent and dependent variables (and any intervening variables) in each hypothesis in #2 above.

4. Provide a conceptual definition for each variable identified in #3.

5. Provide an operational definition for each variable identified in #3. Explain the operational definitions in specific detail. Provide detailed instructions so that another person could carry out the experiment without having to ask you any questions. For example, if the experimenter is going to talk to the subjects, provide a script. Include a step by step outline of everything in the experiment, including a debriefing if deception is used.

6. Identify 1–2 empirical hypotheses linked to the conceptual hypotheses in #2 using your operational definitions.

7. Provide a design for your experiment using design notation (X's and O's). Identify the type of experimental design you are using if you use a standard one.

8. Describe the setting (e.g., when and where such as a student lounge, or a classroom) and units of analysis used.

9. Discuss the reliability of the operational dependent variable and explain how you might check the reliability.

10. Discuss the measurement validity of the operational dependent variable.

11. Discuss at least three forms of internal validity threats that might occur in the experiment (e.g., history, maturation, etc.). Explain in detail how each might lead to false conclusions. Also discuss the experiment's external validity.

Name _____

PRACTICE QUIZ 4, Chapters 7-8 (18 questions)

1. A scholarly article reports that researchers used computers when conducting telephone interviews. Interviewers sat at a computer and read questions off the screen. They entered answers directly into the computers. What are the initials of the technique that was used?

    a. RRT
    b. DDT
    c. RDD
    d. CATI

2. You read about a researcher who had interviewers ask respondents to clarify answers. This is using a:

    a. suppression poll
    b. mutually exclusive
    c. informed consent
    d. floaters
    e. probe

MATCHING
CHOOSE THE TYPE OF QUESTION FROM THE LIST a–h BELOW
FOR DEFINITIONS 3 to 6.

    a. socially desirable question
    b. prestige bias in a question
    c. double-barreled question
    d. leading question
    e. contingency question
    d. threatening question
    f. matrix question

3. Asking about two things in the same question, often creating confusion.

4. Asking a question that many respondents are likely to overreport by giving what they believe to be the normative or "good appearing" answer, and not be entirely truthful.

5. Asking two or more questions, such that answering the first determines which question comes next.

6. Asking about behaviors or opinions associated with a highly-respected groups, person, or publicized position with which respondents will tend to agree.

7. In survey research when a respondent answers many questions by saying "agree" without carefully considering each and giving an honest answer it is called the:

   a. wording effect
   b. order effect
   c. context effect
   d. response set

8. Ten ways have been identified for increasing response rates to mail survey questionnaires. Which of the following is likely to improve responses?

   a. Address an envelope to "occupant" instead of a specific person and send it by bulk mail instead of first class postage.
   b. Make the respondent provide his/her own return envelope and pay the return postage.
   c. Send a very long questionnaire, over 20 pages, with a small print and no "white space."
   d. Include a professionally written letter asking the respondent to complete the questionnaire printed on official letterhead stationary with the researcher clearly identified.
   e. Send questionnaires during major holiday periods.

9. When putting together items in a questionnaire, it is BEST to

   a. Increase social desirability at all times.
   b. Put items about various topics in complete random order, with no logic.
   c. Include clear instructions in a friendly tone that guide a respondent or interviewer.
   d. Use tiny print, single-spaced printing, and no margins or white space to keep printing costs as low as possible.

10. Comparing Mail, Phone, Face-to-Face surveys:

    a. Mail questionnaires have the highest return rate.
    b. Phone interview surveys do not permit the use of probes.
    c. Face-to-face interviews are the most expensive.
    d. Mail questionnaires allow the greatest control over how a respondent answers

11. Jerry Jones the coach at Hometown High school is designing a training program for the track team. He knows that exercise A, B and C are recommended but is not sure which order he should have his team members train in (i.e., A, B, C, or C, A, B, etc). What type of experimental design would he use to test the relative effectiveness of the different training sequences?

    a. One-group pre-test, post-test
    b. Solomon 4-group design
    c. Latin square design
    d. Classical experiment design
    e. Post-test only design

12. The **double-blind** experiment is one in which:

   a. The experimenter's assistant who works with subjects does not know which is the experimental or control group, but the subjects know which group they are in.
   b. The experimental subjects do not know that they are in the experimental group, but the control group subjects know which group they are in.
   c. Neither subjects in any group, nor the experimenter's assistant who works directly with subjects knows which is the experimental or control group.
   d. The control group subjects do not know that they are in the control group, but experimental group subjects know which group they are in.
   e. None of the above.

13. The diagram to the right represents the:

   a. Solomon Four-Group Design
   b. Classical experimental Design
   c. Static Group Comparison
   d. Interrupted Time Series Design
   e. Johnson's Test/Retest model

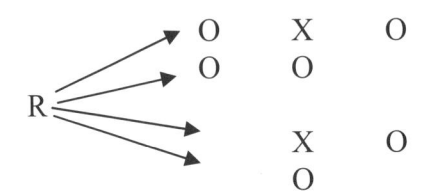

```
              O  X  O
              O     O
          R
                 X  O
                    O
```

USE FOR 14-16

Professor Suchi wanted to replicate findings based on college students that the degree of racial prejudice among White college students would be reduced if they worked on complex tasks in teams with highly capable racial minority students on high school students. He used a **double-blind** procedure with a **classical experimental design**. The control groups worked in all-White teams and the experimental groups were racially mixed. Prejudice was measured with an index of 10 attitude items measured using a 5-point **Likert Scale**. He had five sets of 8 person teams complete a series of complex tasks. Prejudice scores ranged from a low of 0 (non-prejudiced anti-racist attitudes) to 40 (extremely prejudiced and racist attitudes). His results are below, numbers in brackets [] are number of subjects.:

		PRETEST	POSTTEST
a.	Experimental	20 [8]	19 [8]
	Control	10 [8]	10 [8]
b.	Experimental	20 [8]	10 [4]
	Control	21 [8]	19 [8]
c.	Experimental	20 [8]	8 [8]
	Control	21 [8]	9 [9]
d.	Experimental	21 [8]	10 [8]
	Control	20 [8]	20 [8]

14. Which shows support for the hypothesis without internal validity concerns?

15. Which suggests experimental mortality problems?

16. Which suggests selection bias problems?

17. Timothy got a job working for a political candidate who was running for mayor. He decided to apply his knowledge about experiments in his new job and test whether the method of distributing campaign literature caused more people to vote for a candidate. He distributed campaign literature about the candidate to the Riverdale neighborhood in a bright blue envelope that a volunteer hand placed in each person's front door. He distributed the same campaign literature about the candidate to the Golfview neighborhood by mailing it in a plain white envelope that went to each address. He later learned that Riverdale was a low income area of the city that was almost entirely Latino and was 95% Catholic. Golfview was most upper-income area in the city and its residents were 100% white Protestants. What problem with **internal validity** might threaten his ability to trust the experimental results?

    a. Selection Bias
    b. History Effect
    c. Experimental Mortality
    d. Maturation
    e. Testing Effect

18. Yolanda wanted to test the effectiveness of a new 4-hour anger management treatment session at the Purple County social work agency. She first took 24 clients who had been referred for anger management in March and divided them randomly into two groups of 12 clients. One group was assigned to the new 4-hour session, the other group went to a old, traditional anger management session. After clients finished the sessions, she measured the level of anger management skills among all clients in both groups. What **experimental design** did she use?

    a. One-group pre-test, post-test
    b. Solomon 4-group design
    c. Latin square design
    d. Classical experiment design
    e. Two-group posttest only design

CHAPTER 9

NONREACTIVE RESEARCH AND SECONDARY ANALYSIS

LEARNING OBJECTIVES

After studying Chapter 9 you will be able to do the following:
1. Describe the basic logic of nonreactive measurement techniques;
2. Understand the purpose of content analysis and know when it is appropriate to use;
3. Understand coding systems and types of coding used with content analysis;
4. Explain the issue of intercoder reliability;
5. Describe topics appropriate for existing statistics research and potential problems or limitations of it;
6. Discuss validity and reliability issues in existing statistics research;
7. Explain why missing data are a concern in existing statistics research and ways to resolve it.
8. Understand the purposes of secondary data analysis.

KEY TERMS MATCHING DEFINITIONS, CHAPTER 9

1. Another name for non-reactive measures. It emphasize that the people being studied are not aware of it because the measures do not intrude.
2. Nonreactive measures of the residue of the activity of people or what they leave behind.
3. Nonreactive measures of the wear or deterioration on surfaces due to the activity of people.
4. A set of instructions or rules used in content analysis to explain how to systematically convert the symbolic content from text into quantitative data.
5. The process of converting raw information or data into another form for analysis. In content analysis it means a system for determining how to covert symbolic meanings in text into another form, usually numbers
6. A general name for symbolic meaning within a communication medium measured in content analysis.
7. A type of content analysis coding in which a researcher first develops a list of specific words, phrases, or symbols then finds them in a communication medium.
8. A type of content analysis coding in which a researcher identifies subjective meaning such as general themes or motifs in a communication medium.
9. A U.S. government publication that appears annually and contains an extensive complication of statistical tables and information.
10. A survey of a random sample of about 1,500 U.S. adults that has been conducted in most years between 1972 and the present and is available for many researchers to analyze.
11. Measures in which people being studied are unaware that they are in a study.

12. Pages on which a researcher writes down what is coded in <u>content analysis</u>.
13. A method of watching what is happening in a social setting that is highly organized and follows systematic rules for observation and documentation.
14. When a person uses of too many digits in a quantitative measure in an attempt to create the impression that data is accurate or the researcher is highly capable.
15. Research in which one examine patterns of symbolic meaning within text that may be written, audio, visual, or other mediums of communication.

MATCHING KEY TERMS FOR CHAPTER 9

	Accretion Measures		Manifest Coding
	Coding		Nonreactive
	Coding System		Recording Sheet
	Content analysis		*Statistical Abstract of the U.S.*
	Erosion measures		Structured Observation
	Fallacy of misplaced concreteness		Text
	General Social Survey (GSS)		Unobtrusive measures
	Latent coding		

Name _____

Exercise 9.1

Use the CD that comes with the workbook for this exercise and connect to the Internet. Follow the instructions in the workbook preface. From the table of contents, go to Chapter 9.

Locate the *Statistical Abstract of the United States* on the **Internet**. View the most recent on-line version, across the top click on "Print Version" to get a complete set of data. Decide on **three different sections/ chapters** (e.g., crime, education, recreation, etc.) . Select three variables (one from each section) for which data is available on all 50 states [exclude the District of Columbia and U.S. possessions].

You may have to search to find three variables where state is the unit of analysis. Do not use state geographic size or population size as variables. Use the most recent data you can find on the table. Identify the eight states that are highest for each of the three variables.

Put the states in rank order with the actual data number next to each state. Include the table number from which you obtained the data, the year of the data, and the **source of the Table** (e.g., Internet version of *Statistical Abstract* 2005) label it precisely giving the year of the actual data and the specific part of a table's information that you are using.

Be careful not to compare data across states were **standardization** is necessary unless you first standardize the data. For example, if you locate the total amount spent in each state on education but fail to standardize by the state's population, the data is meaningless! Either locate data where this is not a problem or first standardize it yourself. [Standardized data is usually expressed as per capita, a rate per so many 1,000, or in percent]. If you standardize it, note Table sources for both the variable and the "base" for standardization.

If it helps draw lines to connect states that appear on your three tables. Give a short (3-4 sentence) discussion of findings about each table, and which states on top ranked on the three variables. Create a chart with the rankings, data values and your discussion of findings.

Name _____

Exercise 9.2

Standardized data on four variables for 50 States, various sources for about 2002

State	Violent Crime Rate	% in Poverty	% who are Unemployed	% Binge Drinkers
ALABAMA	444.2	14.6	5.3	18.3
ALASKA	563.4	8.3	6.3	20.2
ARIZONA	552.9	13.3	4.7	21.5
ARKANSAS	424.4	18	5.1	19.2
CALIFORNIA	593.4	12.8	5.3	19.1
COLORADO	352.4	9.4	3.7	22
CONNECTICUT	311.1	7.8	3.3	22.3
DELAWARE	599.0	8.1	3.5	21.5
FLORIDA	770.2	12.1	4.8	18.8
GEORGIA	458.8	12.1	4	19.8
HAWAII	262.0	10.6	4.6	18.7
IDAHO	254.9	11.8	5	19.6
ILLINOIS	620.7	11.2	5.4	24.1
INDIANA	357.2	8.7	4.4	19
IOWA	285.6	8.3	3.3	21.9
KANSAS	376.6	9.4	4.3	19.9
KENTUCKY	279.0	13.1	5.5	18.3
LOUISIANA	662.3	17	6	22.3
MAINE	107.8	11.3	4	22.7
MARYLAND	769.8	7.3	4.1	19.5
MASSACHUSETTS	484.4	9.6	3.7	25.9
MICHIGAN	540.3	10.3	5.3	21.9
MINNESOTA	267.5	6.5	3.7	24.1
MISSISSIPPI	343.3	17.6	5.5	18.3
MISSOURI	538.7	9.6	4.7	20
MONTANA	351.5	13.7	4.6	23.2
NEBRASKA	313.9	9.5	3.1	22.8
NEVADA	637.5	8.3	5.3	23.8
NEW HAMPSHIRE	161.2	5.6	3.5	21.9
NEW JERSEY	374.5	7.8	4.2	21.3
NEW MEXICO	739.5	17.8	4.8	22.7
NEW YORK	496.0	14	4.9	19.7
N. CAROLINA	470.2	13.1	5.5	17
N. DAKOTA	78.2	11.9	2.8	29
OHIO	351.3	10.1	4.3	21.7
OKLAHOMA	503.4	14.7	3.8	18.3
OREGON	292.4	11.2	6.3	18.1
PENNSYLVANIA	401.9	9.2	4.7	22.3
RHODE ISLAND	285.2	10.3	4.7	24.2
SOUTH CAROLINA	822.0	13.5	5.4	19.7
SOUTH DAKOTA	177.4	10.2	3.3	24.5
TENNESSEE	716.9	14.2	4.5	16
TEXAS	578.6	15.3	4.8	21.5

UTAH	236.9	9.3	4.4	14.2
VERMONT	106.7	9.9	3.6	23.2
VIRGINIA	291.4	8.7	3.5	17.8
WASHINGTON	345.4	10.8	6.4	18.9
WEST VIRGINIA	234.3	16	4.9	18.2
WISCONSIN	224.9	8.6	4.6	28.3
WYOMING	273.5	9.5	3.9	24.1

List the 10 States that have the Highest Violent Crime Rate	Each of those 10 states' % in poverty	% of those 10 states' workforce that is unemployed	% of those 10 states who are binge drinkers
1.			
2.			
3.			
4.			
5.			
6.			
7.			
8.			
9.			
10.			

List the 10 States that have the Lowest Violent Crime Rate	Each of those 10 states' % in poverty	% of those 10 states' workforce that is unemployed	% of those 10 states who are binge drinkers
1.			
2.			
3.			
4.			
5.			
6.			
7.			
8.			
9.			
10.			

Let us find out whether violent crime rates are associated more strongly with poverty, excessive alcohol consumption, or unemployment. A simple way to do this is to calculate the average rankings for the set of 10 highest ranked and 10 lowest ranked states on violent crime rates. For example, add together the rankings of the 10 highest states for % below poverty and divide by 10. This gives us the average poverty ranking for the set of ten. Do this as well for unemployment and binge drinkers, then repeat to find the average rankings for the set of ten lowest crime states.

For the 10 highest crime states:
    Average ranking on poverty:
    Average ranking on drop-outs
    Average ranking on alcohol consumption
For the 10 lowest crime states:

Average ranking on poverty:
Average ranking on drop-outs
Average ranking on alcohol consumption

Caution: Do not misinterpret this data with the **ecological fallacy** (Chapter 4). If we find that violent crime rates are high in high poverty states, cannot say that poor people are committing violent crime. We only have data on state as the unit of analysis, not the individual. We could say that the high rates of poverty creates a social climate in a state that is associated with higher violent crime rates. Further study is needed to learn the mechanism by which this occurs (e.g., high income people fear very large number of poor people and they commit crime out of fear)

Based on the above simple ranking comparison which one(s) of the three explanatory factors (poverty, unemployment, or excessive alcohol drinking) is most strongly associated to violent crime rates and which one(s) are not very strongly associated? Explain

Name _____

Exercise 9.3

Use the CD that comes with the workbook for this exercise and connect to the Internet. Follow the instructions in the workbook preface. From the table of contents, go to Chapter 9. Click on **County-City Data Book**. Below are the 12 counties with the highest percent of the population living below the poverty rate

County
1. Buffalo, SD   56.9%
2. Shannon, SD   52.3%
3. Starr, TX   50.9%
4. Ziebach, SD   49.9%
5. Todd, SD   48.3%
6. Owsley, KY   45.4%
7. Zavala, TX   41.8%
8. Holmes, MS   41.1%
9. Corson, SD   41.0%
10. East Carroll, LA 40.5%
11. Brooks, TX   40.2%
12. Kalawao, HI   40.1%

Find three other characteristics of these high poverty counties, such as infant morality rate, percent with less than nine years of schooling, etc.

Exercise 9.4

Use the CD that comes with the workbook for this exercise and connect to the Internet. Follow the instructions in the workbook preface. From the table of contents, go to Chapter 9.

Click on **City-County Data Book** and click on scroll down to USA Counties—Over 5,000 data items for all counties. Next click on **USA Counties—Almost 6,000 data items for all counties.** You will see a window and asked to select a state, click on it and you can scroll a list of states. Once the state appears in the window to the right, click on the button next to the open box and you can scroll to a country. Below it is a window that says general profile and you can scroll to topics. Select one state of your choice.

Select a state and one county of that state. Now pick four variables for the county, click on Compare to see how that county compares to others of the same state. Also compare that county with state totals for the four variables.

State: _____   Country: _____

Four variables you picked:
1. _____
2. _____
3. _____
4. _____

Your findings: _____

_____

Exercise 9.5

Use the CD that comes with the workbook for this exercise and connect to the Internet. Follow the instructions in the workbook preface. From the table of contents, go to Chapter 9.

Click on **Statistical Resources on the Web, Sociology**. Select three of the highlighted items on the long list. Once you get "into" the locations, find specific statistical data on a topic.

Print out a copy of the data and write one 1 page paper based on each data set you look at. For example, I looked at Hate Crimes and saw FBI statistics on the number of hate crime victims. I noticed that the number of Anti-Hispanic hate crime victims and the number of Anti-Asian hate crime victims was not the same as the relative size of the Asian and Latino populations in the United States. I won't tell you what I learned—you can check it out to see which group was the victimized more.

CHAPTER 10

ANALYZING QUANTITATIVE DATA

LEARNING OBJECTIVES

After studying Chapter 10 you will be able to do the following:
1. Describe the process of coding quantitative data and methods for cleaning the coded data;
2. Construct a frequency distribution, describe its purpose, and properly interpret or read different forms of the frequency distribution;
3. Calculate the three measures of central tendency and describe their characteristics;
4. Understand the concept of variation and interpret the standard deviation;
5. Understand the use of the z-score and calculate both the z-score of a score and the score corresponding to a z-score if given the mean and standard deviation;
6. Construct a scattergram and recognize various bivariate relationships in a scattergram;
7. Construct a bivariate percentaged table, describe the parts of a table, and properly interpret a simple bivariate percentaged cross-tabulation;
8. Interpret the meaning for a relationship of specific correlation coefficients;
9. Construct trivariate percentaged tables, understand the concept of statistical control and interpret trivariate tables in terms of the elaboration paradigm;
10. Understand the concept of statistical significance, the basic logic of Type I and Type II errors, and interpret the meaning of various levels of significance.

KEY TERMS MATCHING DEFINITIONS, CHAPTER 10

1. A document that describes the procedure for coding variables and their location in a format for computers.
2. A table that shows the cross-tabulation of two or more variables. Usually it shows bivariate quantitative data for variables in the form of percentages across rows or down columns for the categories of one variable.
3. A measure of central tendency for one variable that indicates the most frequent or common score.
4. A measure of central tendency for one variable indicating the point or score at which half the cases are higher and half are lower.
5. A measure of central tendency for one variable that indicates the arithmetic average, i.e., the sum of all scores divided by the total number of scores.
6. A measure of dispersion for one variable indicating the highest and lowest scores.
7. A measure of dispersion for one variable that indicates the percentage of cases at or below a score or point.
8. A measure of dispersion for one variable that indicates an average distance between the scores and the mean.

9. Paper with a printed grid into which a researcher records information so that it can be easily entered into a computer. It is an alternative to direct-entry method and using optical-scan sheets.
10. A display of numerical information on one variable that divides a circle into fractions by lines representing the proportion of cases in the variable's attributes.
11. Placing data for two variables in a contingency table to show the number or percentage of cases at the intersection of categories of the two variables.
12. The center part of a contingency table. It contains all the cells, but not the totals or labels.
13. A part of the body of a table, in a contingency table that shows the distribution of cases into categories of variables as a specific number or percentage.
14. A way to locate a score in a distribution of scores by determining the number of standard deviations it is above or below the mean or arithmetic average.
15. A "third" variable that shows whether or not a bivariate relationship holds up to alternative explanations. It can occur before or between other variables.
16. A method of entering data into a computer by typing data without code or optical scan sheets.
17. A system for describing patterns evident among tables when bivariate contingency table is compared with partials after the control variable has been added.
18. A pattern in the elaboration paradigm in which the partials show the same relationship as in a bivariate contingency table of the independent and dependent variable alone.
19. A pattern in the elaboration paradigm in which the bivariate contingency table shows a relationship, but the partials show no relationship and the control variable is intervening in the causal explanation.
20. A pattern in the elaboration paradigm in which the bivariate contingency table shows a relationship, but the partials show no relationship and the control variable occurs prior to the independent variable.
21. A pattern in the elaboration paradigm in which no relationship appears in a bivariate contingency table, but the partials show a relationship between the variables.
22. A pattern in the elaboration paradigm in which the bivariate contingency table shows a relationship. One of the partial tables shows the relationship, but other tables do not.
23. Cleaning data using a computer in which the researcher looks at the combination of categories for two variables for logically impossible cases.
24. Cleaning data using a computer in which the researcher looks for responses or answer categories that cannot have cases.
25. A diagram to display the statistical relationship between two variables based on plotting each case's values for both of the variables.
26. The absence of a statistical relationship between two variables, i.e., when knowing the values on one variable provides no information about the values one will find on another variable. There is no association between them.
27. Statistical measures that deal with one variable only.
28. In contingency tables for three variables, tables that show the association between the independent and dependent variables for each category of a control variable.

29. A display of <u>quantitative data</u> for one variable in the form of rectangles where longer rectangles indicate more cases in a variable category. Usually it is used with discrete data and there is a small space between rectangles. They can have a horizonal or vertical orientation.
30. The totals in a <u>contingency table</u>, outside the <u>body of a table</u>.
31. A set of numbers researchers use as a simple way to measure the degree to which a <u>statistical relationship</u> results from random factors rather the existence of a true relationship among <u>variables</u>.
32. A distribution of cases among the categories of a <u>variable</u> which is not <u>normal</u>, i.e., not a "bell shape." Instead of an equal number of cases on both ends, more are at one of the extremes.
33. A table that shows the distribution of cases into the categories of one <u>variable</u>, i.e., the number or percent of cases in each category.
34. A graph of connected points showing the distribution of how many cases fall into each category of a <u>variable</u>.
35. Statistical measures that involve two <u>variables</u> only.
36. Expressing whether or not two or more <u>variables</u> affect one another based on the use of elementary applied mathematics, i.e., whether there is an <u>association</u> between them or <u>independence</u>.
37. An <u>association</u> between two <u>variables</u> that is positive or negative across the attributes or levels of the <u>variables</u>. When plotted in a <u>scattergram</u> the basic pattern of the <u>association</u> forms a straight line, not a curve or other pattern.
38. A relationship between two <u>variables</u> such that as the values of one <u>variable</u> increase, the values of the second show a changing pattern, e.g., first decrease then increase then decrease. It is not a <u>linear relationship</u>.
39. A general type of simple statistics used by researchers to describe basic patterns in the <u>data</u>.
40. A "bell-shaped" <u>frequency polygon</u> for a distribution of cases, with a peak in the center and identical curving slopes on either side of the center. It is the distribution of many natural-occurring phenomena and is a basis of much statistical theory.
41. The logical error of falsely accepting the <u>null hypothesis</u>.
42. The logical error of falsely rejecting the <u>null hypothesis</u>.
43. A way to discuss the likelihood that a finding or <u>statistical relationship</u> in a <u>sample</u> results is due to the random factors rather than due to the existence of an actual relationship in the entire <u>population</u>.

Student Workbook for Neuman, *Basics of Social Research*, 2e   97

Name _____

MATCHING KEY TERMS FOR CHAPTER 10

	Bar chart		Marginals
	Bivariate statistics		Mean
	Body of a table		Median
	Cell of a table		Mode
	Code sheets		Normal distribution
	Codebook		Partials
	Contingency cleaning		Percentile
	Contingency table		Pie chart
	Control variable		Possible code cleaning
	Covariation		Range
	Cross-tabulation		Replication pattern
	Curvilinear relationship		Scattergram
	Descriptive statistics		Skewed distribution
	Direct entry method		Specification pattern
	Elaboration paradigm		Standard deviation
	Explanation pattern		Statistical significance
	Frequency distribution		Suppressor variable pattern
	Frequency polygon		Type I error
	Independence		Type II error
	Interpretation pattern		Univariate statistics
	Level of statistical significance		Z score
	Linear relationship		

Name _____

Exercise 10.1

This exercise uses the CD that comes with the workbook. Open SPSS on your computer [how to install/run SPSS is discussed in the front section of this workbook].

In the opening screen of SPSS, click on the button that says **Open an Existing Data Source**. Pick the file called **RaceEthnic**. (See Appendix B of this Workbook for a description of the data file).

1. Click on the **View** button at the top and select **Variables**. Look at the 44 variables available for analysis. You may wish to expand the Label column to read the entire question for a variable. Note which variables are nominal, ordinal, or scale (interval/ratio)in the Measure column.

2. Click on **Analyze** and Select **Descriptive Statistics** and within it **Frequencies.** In the box that opens, select four variables of your choice in the left open window with a list of variables. Highlight them (one at a time) and click on the arrow button between the right and left open windows to pull it into the right window. When you are done click the **OK** button.

3. Look at the frequency distribution for your four variables.

4. Now click **Analyze** and Select **Descriptive Statistics** and within it **Frequencies** again. You should see you four variables still moved over to the open window on the left for analysis. This time, Click the Charts button and select pie charts. Click on the continue button then the OK button.

You should see the same frequency distribution but in addition colored pie charts as well. The pie charts contain the same information as the frequency tables, but display it in a different format. You can print this if you want by selecting the Print option under the File Button (top on far left). When you are done click the x or close button on the far upper right corner. You will get a question asking you whether you want to save the contents of the output viewer. Click on **No**.

5. Now we are going to create a cross tabulation or bivariate percentage table. To do this return to **Analyze** and Select **Descriptive Statistics.** This time you will notice that there are two open variable selection windows to the right. One is for a row variable the other for a column variable.

Decide on two variables this time. Make the column variable your Independent Variable and the row variable your Dependent Variable. Create a hypothesis for your two variables, (e.g. the greater one's educational degree, the less likely they are to own a pistol). Put you Independent Variable as the Column and the Depenent Variable as the row in your table.

Note: Some variables are nominal so the hypothesis should reflect their status (e.g., male are more likely than females to own pistols). Some variable have many categories (i.e., education, income, age) and do not work well for cross tabulation. You may want to return to step 1 to see how the number of categories a variable has. Once you select you column and row variable, click on the OK button. The data are in raw form, i.e., not percentaged. Close the viewer and do not save the output.

6. Return to **Analyze** and Select **Descriptive Statistics** and **Crosstabs.** The variables you selected should still be in two open variable selection windows, for row and column. This time we want to create a table with that is percentaged by column. Click on the **Cells** button (lower part of widow in center). Select **Column** under Percentages (to lower right). Click on the Continue then OK the buttons when done.

You can now see the cross tabulation of your two variables percentaged by column.

7. We want to save the output this time. To save the output, click on **File** (upper left button) and select **Export.** The only export format that keeps everything clearly is HTML, so select HTML under file type (right, bottom). You will have to give the output a name and location using the BROWSE button.

8. Save your output and print it out. Write your hypothesis and discuss what you saw in the Table.

Name _____

Exercise 10.2

This is a continuation of Exercise 10.1. Again go to SPSS and open the **RaceEthnic** data file.

1. This time begin by creating six bivariate hypotheses that you can test with the data. Select two dependent variables and three independent variables that go with the two dependent variables. You may want to review the available variables in the data file before creating the hypotheses. Write your hypothesis below.

    1. _____

    2. _____

    3. _____

    4. _____

    5. _____

    6. _____

2. Now you want to create a bivariate table for each hypothesis, following the steps from Exercise 10.1 number 6 for creating Crosstabs. Follow the steps up through clicking on **Cells** and selecting Column percents, then Continue.

Stop. Before clicking ok click on **Statistics**. A window will open that offers you many types of statistics. Correlations will not be appropriate unless both your variables are ratio level. You can look at all the choices, but for this exercise just select **Chi-Square**. After you select it then select the Continue and OK buttons.

3. Everything should look similar to the Tables created in Exercise 10.1, except at the bottom of each table there is a Chi-Square Table. You may see several things in the Table.

First, you will see the Pearson Chi-Square value and its df (degrees of freedom). These are always reported for Chi-Square tests. In the same row is something called Asymp. Sig. (2-sided). This is the probability for a test of statistical significance. Information from it is always reported, but usually as a level of statistical significance. Here is a simple rule to use when reporting levels of significance.

> **.001 level if significance probability is .000–.001**
> **.01 level if significance probability is .002–.010**
> **.05 level if significance probability is .011–.050**
> **not significant if significance probability is .051 or larger.**

Lastly, you may see a warning message or note below the Table that some cells had an expected count of less than 5. Chi-square is calculated by creating expected values for each cell (see textbook) and if the expected value of a cell is under 5, Chi-square may not work properly.

4. Print your six tables and write up a short description of the results of each, including Chi-Square.

Name _____

Exercise 10.3

This is exercise assumes you mastered the skills from the two previous exercises. It uses the CD. Again go to SPSS. This time open the **Gender** data file.

1. First, we will modify categories of two variables. Locate the variable for Region (Variable 15) the region of the interview based on U.S. Census regions. It has 9 categories:

   1 New England
   2 Mid-Atlantic
   3 East North Central
   4 West North Central
   5 South Atlantic
   6 East South Central
   7 East South Central
   8 Mountain
   9 Pacific

We want to simply this variable and collapse the nine regions into four regions: Northeast, Midwest, South, West. Select **Transform** from the buttons along the top. Select **Recode** and into a **different variable.** Locate Region in the open left window and use the arrow button to put it in the open right window.

Give the new variable the name Region2 and the label Recoded Region. Now find the **Old and New Values** button (about the middle of the widow) and click on it. A new window opens. It asks for **Old Values** on the upper left and wants you to enter **New Values** on the upper right. Old Values are those that the original variable Region had (see above). Let us say we want to combine 1 and 2 (New England and Mid-Atlantic) into a new region Northwest. Put 1 in Old value and 1 in New Value. Click on the **Add** button when done. You will see a notation 1 --> 1 appear. Next Put 2 in the Old Value and 1 in the New Value box and click **Add**. It now shows 2 -->1. Thus, any case that had 1 or 2 will become 1 in the new Variable Region2.

Repeat the process recoding Old Values 3 and 4 into 2, Old Values 5, 6 and 7 into 3, Old Values 8, 9 into 4. Note that if you make a mistake, you can highlight the Recode open window with arrows and remove it. When you are done, click on the **Continue** then the **OK** buttons. Scroll to the bottom and see the new variable on the variable list, as variable 48. If we left it here, we would have to remember that 1 was Northeast, 2 Midwest, etc. To add value labels, go to the column that says **Values** for the new variable Recode2 and click on it. It will open up a new window called Value Labels. Enter the value 1, the value label Northeast and click on the **Add** button. Repeat the process, 2 = Midwest, 3 = South, 4 = West. Click on **OK** when done.

2. Now we are going to use our new Region2 variable in a Crosstab. Among the top button click on **Analyze,** then select **Descriptive Statistics** and **Crosstabs.** Enter REGION2 as your column variable and RAPEAB (the variable right above it) as your row variable. Click on **Cells** and column percentage, **Statistics** and Chi-Square then OK as in Exercise 10.2. See whether abortion in the case of a woman becoming pregnant as the result of rape differs across the four regions of the U.S. Print the Table.

3. You might wonder whether another variable is also at work. Perhaps we should control on a third variable and make a multi-variate analysis with the Elaboration Paradigm. Go back and click on **Analyze,** then select **Descriptive Statistics** and **Crosstabs.** You should see REGION2 and RAPEAB still there. Notice a third open window beneath the words Layer 1 of 1. Locate Religion among the variable and click on the arrow button next to the third open window to put it into the active area. Click OK and look at the Table. The table is large and complex. It begins by showing the percentage of Protestants who say yes or no in each region, then examines many other religious groups. The Chi-Square has a warning that many of the cells have expected values of under 5. Do not save the output. If we wanted to combine religious groups into a smaller number for analysis, we would follow the same procedure that we used to create REGION2.

4. Let us try another Independent variable (for the column). Go back and click on **Analyze,** then select **Descriptive Statistics** and **Crosstabs.** Your previous work should still be showing. Highlight the REGION2 and RELGION variable and remove it (note the arrow button points in a reverse direction and puts it back in the list of variables). Leave RAPEAB as the Row Variable. Now select the variable that says Would you be for or against sex education in the schools. It only has two values. Use the arrow button to pull it into the open window for as Column Variable then click **OK**. This creates a bivariate Table. Is the Chi-Square statistically significant? What does the Table show? Print the Table and provide an discussion of the results.

5. Now we can add a control variable to the table created in step 4. Go back and click on **Analyze,** then select **Descriptive Statistics** and **Crosstabs.** Your previous work should still be showing. Select Respondent's Sex as your control variable. Click the OK button and look at the Table. It shows the relationship between opinion about sex education by Abortion position when a woman is pregnant as the result of rape for men and for women. Look at the Table carefully. Now go to the Chi-Square results are they similar or different from the bivariate case in step 4 above? Print the Table. In terms of the Elaboration paradigm, what is the effect of gender (or sex) on the bivariate relationship between sex education opinion and stand on abortion in the case of rape? Does gender have an impact?

6. Create your own bivariate hypothesis using variables in the Gender data file. After you create a bivariate table, add a control variable of your choice and see its effect. Caution, it is usually best to select control variables that do has 2 to 4 categories.

Name _____

Exercise 10.4

WHAT DOES LIVING IN A HIGH INCOME COUNTRY MEAN?

The data below come from the World Bank as of 2004.

Countries 2004	Per Person Income in US dollars	per 1000 Internet Users	Infant Death Rate	Average Life Expect
1. Australia	27,070	646	5	80
2. Austria	32,280	477	5	79
3. Belgium	31,280	403	4	79
4. Canada	28,310	626	5	80
5. Denmark	40,750	696	4	77
6. Finland	32,880	629	3	79
7. France	30,370	414	4	80
8. Germany	30,690	500	4	78
9. Greece	16,730	177	4	79
10. Ireland	34,310	265	5	78
11. Italy	26,280	501	4	80
12. Japan	37,050	587	3	82
13. Luxembourg	56,380	597	5	78
14. Netherlands	32,130	614	5	79
15. Norway	51,810	390	4	80
16. Portugal	14,220	281	4	77
17. S. Korea,	14,000	657	5	77
18. Singapore	24,760	571	3	79
19. Spain	21,530	336	3	80
20. Sweden	35,840	756	3	80
21. Switzerland	49,600	474	5	81
22. United Kingdom	33,630	628	5	79
23. United States	41,441	630	7	77

The standardized data above show four variables for 23 high income countries.

USE THE ABOVE DATA:

1. Rank order the countries by total income per person.

2. Rank order country by Internet users, Infant Death rate and Life Expectancy.

3. Focus on the five richest nation or five lowest nations in the list relate to rank on technology use (Internet Users) and health (Deaths of Infants and Life Expectancy)? Does being the richest among the world's rich nation always predict better health and technology access? Which of the 10 richest countries best fits this prediction? Which one seems to be an exception? Many people drop Luxembourg because it is so tiny with just 474,413 people, does this change your findings? Write up your findings.

4. A highly desirable nation is one with high income, good health care, and technology access, so one might think such a nation would attract many immigrants. Go to the CIA Fact Book (see link on CD http://www.cia.gov/cia/publications/factbook/index.html go to each of these 23 countries and click on People, then and find the net migration rate (number of people entering a country—number leaving). Some of these countries have no one entering others have a many more people per 1,000 population of the country entering than leaving. See whether being "desirable" predicts the amount of immigration into a nation. Show your new variable and write up your findings.

Name _____

PRACTICE QUIZ 5, Chapters 9-10 (12 questions)

1. Which of the following measure(s) of central tendency are most affected by a very extreme value?

    a. Mean
    b. Median
    c. Mode
    d. a and b equally
    e. b and c equally

2. If the standard deviation equals zero we know:

    a. There is no dispersion of the data
    b. The data are homogenous
    c. The mean is a good measure of central tendency
    d. All of the above

3. Given the following table of hypothetical data relating age to employment status, which of the following conclusion(s) can be drawn?

    Table 1: Frequency Table of Age by Prestige of Job for 3,600 adults

	JOB PRESTIGE		
Age	High	Medium	Low
21-40	100	300	800
41-50	300	700	500
51-70	600	200	100
TOTAL	1000	1200	1400

    a. There is a negative association between age and employment status
    b. As age increases so does the employment status
    c. There is a positive association between age and employment status
    d. a and b only are correct
    e. b and c only are correct

4. What is the MEAN of the following set of scores? 3, 6, 1, 10

    a. 4
    b. 4.5
    c. 5
    d. 6
    e. 7

5. Henri Hendersen weighs 190 pounds. The mean weight of men in Henri's dorm is 170 pounds, the median is 175 feet and the mode is 180 pounds. The standard deviation for men in the dorm is 10 pounds. What is Henri's z score on the distribution of men's height in his dorm?

   a. zero
   b. 1
   c. 2
   d. 2.5
   e. -1

6. The term "possible code cleaning" refers to:

   a. Throwing out all cases with any missing information
   b. The outside margin of a questionnaire with spaces corresponding to data card columns
   c. Examining the distribution of categories for legal categories (e.g. if Male =1 and Female = 0, check that no 7's are punched)
   d. Compare answers to two different variables for logically Impossible combinations (e.g. males listed as given birth to children)
   e. Marking a sheet with a black pencil so that the sheet can be "read" by a special machine and the information put into a computer

7. What is the MEDIAN of the following values: 8, 12, 9, 15, 17, 11, 13, 14, 7.

   a. 12
   b. 17
   c. 4.5
   d. 5
   e. There is no median in this data

8. Raw Frequency of population per MD and Infant Mortality in the world's 25 richest nations.

Number of People per Medical Doctor	Infant Mortality Rate (Deaths per 1,000 Births)			
	5-6	7	8	9-10
700 +	1	2	1	0
600-699	1	2	0	0
500-599	0	0	1	1
400-499	1	2	2	1
200-399	0	2	4	4
TOTAL	3	8	8	6

Looking at the table above, which is the most accurate interpretation of what it shows?

a. The fewer people each MD has to serve, the lower the infant mortality rate, but the relationship is moderate.
b. There is no relationship between number of MD's and infant mortality.
c. The more people each MD has to serve, the lower the infant mortality rate, but the relationship is moderate.
d. The more people each MD has to serve, the higher the infant mortality rate, but the relationship is moderate.

9. The table below is a Raw Frequency of population per MD and Infant Mortality in the world's 25 poorest nations. Looking at the table below, which is the most accurate interpretation of what it shows?

Infant Death Rate per 1,000 births	**Population per Medical Doctor**			
	under 3,000	3,000 to 10,000	10,000 to 19,000	20,000 and more
120 or more	0	0	1	6
100-119	0	0	2	2
80-99	1	4	1	0
under 80	4	4	0	0
Total	5	8	4	9

a. The fewer people each MD has to serve, the lower the infant mortality rate.
b. There is no relationship between number of MD's and infant mortality.
c. The more people each MD has to serve, the higher the infant mortality rate.
d. The more people each MD has to serve, the lower the infant mortality rate.
e. a and c

10. There is a negative relationship between smoking cigarettes and level of education. When age (age categories 16-26, 27-44, 45-58. 59 and older) is a control variable, the relationship disappears in two partials (48-58 and 59 and older), but remains the same in the other partials. Using the elaboration paradigm, what do we say is going on?

    a. Replication
    b. Interpretation
    c. Elaboration
    d. Specification
    e. Suppressor Variable

11. Harry Hogshead examined the FBI Crime Reports and claimed that the number of sexual assaults increased. After examining the same reports more carefully, Cheryl Certsbreath claimed that the reporting the crimes, not the incidence of sexual assault itself, increased. The FBI reports measure crimes reported to police. This illustrates:

    a. The problem of reliability in using existing statistics
    b. The problem of validity in using existing statistics
    c. The need to replicate existing statistics
    d. The ecological fallacy
    e. All of the above

12. Jose Garcia has a list of measures on the Hispanic influence in Atlanta. He asked you to identify the one that is **NOT** an unobtrusive measure, which one is it?

    a. The wear on novels in the Atlanta Public Library written in Spanish
    b. Walking down a street in Atlanta and noticing the store signs are in Spanish
    c. A list of votes supporting bills on bilingual education in the Georgia state legislature with the area represented by the legislator noted.
    d. A box of 300 letters that were written by Chicanos living in Atlanta to relatives living in Mexico between 1980 and 1985.
    e. A 4-page questionnaire in Spanish distributed to residents of a neighborhood.

CHAPTER 11

FIELD RESEARCH

LEARNING OBJECTIVES

After studying Chapter 11 you will be able to do the following:
1. Explain when field research is an appropriate research technique;
2. Describe the steps in conducting a field research study;
3. Discuss the issues of site selection and access in field research;
4. Explain how field researchers maintain social relations in the field setting and several approaches they adopt to gather information;
5. Discuss the various social roles and degrees of involvement a field researcher can adopt;
6. Describe techniques for resolving conflicts in the field and writing field notes;
7. Discuss reliability and validity in field research;
8. Describe differences between field research and survey research interviews;
9. Explain the kind of questions asked in field research interviewing and use of informants;
10. Discuss at least two ethical issues specific to field research.

KEY TERMS MATCHING DEFINITIONS, CHAPTER 11

1. This happens when a researcher in field research gets overly involved and loses all distance or objectivity and becomes like the people being studied.
2. When a field researcher takes what he/she sees at face value and does not question what people say and he/she focuses only on the immediate details in the field setting..
3. The principle that researchers should examine events as they occur in natural, everyday on-going social settings.
4. A technique in field research in which researchers maintain relations in a field site by pretending to be interested and excited by the activities of those studied even though they are actually uninterested or very bored.
5. Techniques in field research used by researchers to make the people being studied feel more comfortable with the research process and to help them accept the researcher's presence.
6. A technique in field research in which researchers study a field site by mentally adjusting to "see" it for the first time or as an outsider.
7. Notes taken in field research that attempt to include all details and specifics of what the researcher heard or saw in a field site. They are written in a way that permits multiple interpretations later.
8. In field research, what a researcher inconspicuously writes while in the field site on whatever is convenient in order to "jog the memory" later.
9. The written notes a qualitative researcher takes during data collection and afterwards to develop concepts, themes, or preliminary generalizations.

10. The one or more natural locations where a researcher conducts field research.
11. A way to achieve reliability of data in field research in which the researcher cross-checks and verifies qualitative data using multiple sources of information.
12. A type of question asked in early in field research. The researcher seeks basic information (e.g., who, what, when, where) about the field site.
13. A type of question in field research interviews in which the researcher attempts to verify the correctness of placing terms or events into the categories of the meaning system used by people being studied.
14. A type of interview question asked late in field research in which the researcher verifies the distinctions among categories in the meaning system of people being studied.
15. A way to demonstrate the authenticity and trustworthiness of a field research study by having the people who were studied, i.e., members, read and confirm as being true that which the researcher has reported.
16. An approach to social science that combines philosophy, social theory, and method to study common sense knowledge. Researchers using it study ordinary social interaction in small-scale settings to reveal the rules that people use to construct and maintain their everyday social reality.
17. An approach to field research that emphasizes providing a very detailed description of a different culture from the viewpoint of an insider in that culture in order to permit a greater understanding of it.
18. When a researcher in field research learns of illegal, unethical or immoral actions by the people in the field site that is not widely known.
19. A way to demonstrate the authenticity and trustworthiness of a field research study by showing that the researcher's descriptions of the field site matches those of the members from the site and that the researcher was not a major disturbance.
20. A type of group interview in which an interviewer asks open ended questions to a small group. Answers are obtained in an open discussion among group members.
21. A way to achieve reliability of data in field research in which a researcher examines the data for plausibility and sees whether the data form a coherent picture, based on everything that has been learned about a person or event and trying to avoid common forms of deception or misleading information.

Name _____

MATCHING KEY TERMS FOR CHAPTER 11

	Analytic Memos		Field site
	Appearance of interest		Focus group
	Attitude of Strangeness		Go native
	Contrast question		Guilty Knowledge
	Descriptive question		Internal Consistency
	Direct Observation Notes		Jotted notes
	Ecological validity		Member validation
	Ethnography		Naturalism
	Ethnographic Fallacy		Normalize social research
	Ethnomethodology		Structural question
	External Consistency		

Name _____

Exercise 11.1

Do this exercise in teams or individually. It gives you minimal "first hand" experience in field research. Conduct 4 hours of field observation and take detailed field notes. If your instructor has you work in teams, all team members should observe the same setting at different times. Observe on three different days with each observation period at least one hour long. A key to success is to think about the site you select, put effort and involvement into observation, take detailed and in-depth notes, and seriously reflect about the experience. Separate your field notes as described in the textbook and make sparing use of "jotted notes."

Part 1: Locate a setting and gain access. Write a 1–2 paragraph explanation of why the site was chosen, whether the first site was selected, and if not why. Also discuss any access problems encountered. Characteristics of a good site for observation include:
1) it has 1–2 small to moderate sized rooms;
2) it has 5 to 25 people;
3) there are few college students there;
4) it is a new and unknown place, you "should" feel a little uncomfortable;
5) people at the site talk to each other and have interacted with each other in the past.

Better settings are:
small churches, court rooms, civic clubs, bingo parlors, bowling alleys, small local bars or restaurants, beauty parlors or barber shops, small town banks, and small work settings.
Difficult settings are:
large supermarkets, shopping malls, large public waiting areas, fast food outlets, large health clubs or sports centers, libraries, and most places on a college campus.

Describe the setting in detail in 1–2 pages. Be explicit and describe the color, size, appearance, odors, sounds, etc. For example, instead of, "there was a cross in the front of the church" say "at the front of the church, backed by a stained class window through which the morning sun shone, there was a gold colored cross about 20' tall and about 10' wide which hung just above the alter with wires attached to the ceiling."

Part 2: Conduct field observation and apply techniques described in the textbook. Observe very closely, adopt an attitude of strangeness, and take only very few "jotted notes" in the field, write up extensive field notes shortly after leaving the field. Separate the field notes into three sections:
1) direct observation,
2) interpretation,
3) analytic notes/personal journal.

Always include the date, time, and name of the observer at the top of each page of field notes and attach the "jotted notes" to the field notes they correspond to. Conduct a short (10 minute) "unstructured interview" with an "informant."

HINTS FOR WRITING GOOD FIELD NOTES

> Be specific. Do not say, "Most people wore blue jeans." Instead say, "I saw five people in blue jeans, and two people whose pants I could not see."
>
> Be clear. Do not say, "It was intense" or "nice." Describe what you actually saw/heard or saw.
>
> Use precise terms. Also do not say "This store's attitude towards..." Stores do no have attitudes, people do.
>
> Do not make unfounded assumptions. For example, do not say, "a group of 10 college students arrived together" say "a group of 10 people who were 18–22 years old arrived together at about 10:15." Only call individuals college students if you have specific information
>
> Be explicit. Assume you are writing for a reader who knows nothing about the social or physical setting. Do not say, it was a "typical student bar" describe it in detail as if the reader has never been to such a place.

Part 3: Write a 1–2 page summary-evaluation of the observation. It should include:
- how you would do things differently if you were to begin over again,

- types of things you think you missed in the field notes

- themes or ideas you would focus on if you were to continue the observation for an additional 20 hours, your personal feelings, insights, reactions or thoughts while doing the observation,

- your overall evaluation of what you learned, or failed to learn, from this experience and how you might use the learning elsewhere.

Student Workbook for Neuman, *Basics of Social Research*, 2e   115

Name _____

Exercise 11.2

Go to your college library and locate a scholarly article in which field research was used. Two especially good journals to look are The Journal of Contemporary Ethnography and Qualitative Inquiry, although you may find them in other journals (look at the references for Chapter 11). Attach a photocopy of the first page of the article and give a full citation of it:

1. Describe the main topic of the study:

2. What is the field setting or site where most observation took place?

3. How long did the observation take place?

4. What types of people or social interaction did the researcher focus on?

5. How did the field researcher gain access to the field setting?

6. What was the researcher's social role the field setting?

7. What methodological issues does the researcher address?

8. Identify two major themes or generalizations from the study.

Name _____

Exercise 11.3

Use the computer CD that comes with the workbook for this exercise and connect to the Internet. Follow the instructions in the workbook preface. From the table of contents, go to Chapter 11.

Go to Center for Ethnography of Everyday Life and once at their web site, click on Publications. Select a research paper and read it. Note that the web site offers abstracts only for some papers, but for others it gives you the full paper. Answer the same eight questions as listed in Exercise 11.2 above.

Chapter 12

HISTORICAL-COMPARATIVE RESEARCH

LEARNING OBJECTIVES

After studying Chapter 12 you will be able to do the following:
1. Identify the types of research questions or topics for which H-C research is most suited;
2. List the similarities between historical-comparative research and field research, as well as, unique features of H-C research;
3. Describe the sequence of steps involved in historical-comparative research;
4. Distinguish primary from secondary historical evidence and internal from external criticism;
5. Recognize possible errors or fallacies that may occur in H-C research;
6. Discuss issues a researcher faces when "reading" secondary material;
7. Understand the problem of equivalence and recognize more than one form of the equivalence problem;
8. Describe Galton's Problem and discuss the issues involved in using a culture versus the nation-state as a unit of analysis.

KEY TERMS MATCHING DEFINITIONS, CHAPTER 12

1. A technique in comparative research for checking lexicon equivalence. A researcher translates spoken or written text from an original language into a second language, then translates the same text in the second language back into the original language, then compares two original language texts.
2. How historical researchers establish the authenticity and credibility of primary sources and determine its accuracy as an account of what occurred.
3. In historical research, a way to check the authenticity of primary sources by accurately locating the place and time of its creation (e.g., it is not a forgery).
4. An extensive catalog and comprehensive collection of ethnographies on many cultures (mostly pre-literate) that permits a researcher to compare across cultural units.
5. The issue in historical-comparative research of whether social roles, norms or situations across different cultures or historical periods are equivalent or can be compared.
6. In historical-comparative research, the issue of whether the same ideas or concepts occur or can be used to represent phenomena across divergent cultural or historical settings.
7. Finding equivalent words or phrases to express the identical meaning in different languages or in the translation from one language to another (see back translation).
8. In historical-comparative research, creating or locating measures that will accurately represent the same construct or variable in divergent cultural or historical settings.

9. <u>Qualitative data</u> or <u>quantitative data</u> used in historical research. It is evidence about past social life or events that was created and used by the persons who actually lived in the historical period.
10. In comparative research, the problem of finding correlations or <u>associations</u> among <u>variables</u> or characteristics in multiple cases or units, when the characteristics actually diffused from a single unit or have a common origin. Thus, a researcher cannot really treat the multiple units (e.g., countries, cultures) as being wholly separate.
11. <u>Qualitative data</u> and <u>quantitative data</u> used in historical research. Information about events or settings are documented or written latter by historians or others who did not directly participate in the events or setting.
12. The words or writings of people about their life experiences after some time has passed. The writings are based on a memory of the past, but may be stimulated by a review of past objects, photos, personal notes or belongings.
13. A special type of <u>existing statistics research</u> used in historical research because the files, records, or documents are maintained in a relatively consistent manner over a period of time.
14. A type of <u>recollection</u> in which a researcher interviews a person about the events, beliefs or feelings in the past that the person directly experienced.

MATCHING KEY TERMS FOR CHAPTER 12

	Back translation		Lexicon equivalence
	Conceptual Equivalence		Measurement equivalence
	Contextual Equivalence		Oral history
	External criticism		Primary sources
	Galton's Problem		Recollections
	Human Relations Area Files (HRAF)		Running records
	Internal Criticism		Secondary Sources

Name _____

Exercise 12.1

Go to the library and read **two daily newspapers** for every day of the month in which **your mother or father was born** and **two news magazines (e.g., Time, Newsweek, U.S. News and World Reports, etc.) for the same month**.

- What has remained unchanged and is the same today?
- What was the most dramatic technological changes you notice?
- What was the most dramatic social-moral-value change you notice?
- What political changes or changes in references to geographic places do you notice?
- Did you find any statements or projections about the future which you know to be false?

Exercise 12.2

1. Find a college student or adult to interview who lived at least five years in a different culture and who has lived in your culture for one year or more. Conduct an informal interview with him or her regarding differences and similarities in the cultures.

2. Go to the library and look up a general discussion of the culture. Write a two page comparison of how what you read compares with what the interview revealed.

3. Locate a grandparent, aunt/uncle, or neighbor who is a least 65 years old and tell them that you would like to conduct a 45 minute interview with him or her. Bring along a tape recorder (and batteries or tape as is necessary) and ask him/her to describe everyday life prior to his/her 20th birthday, ask general questions and probe for specifics, but make sure that they do most of the talking. Take the tape recorded interview and listen to the tape to identify major changes between the world they grew up in and today. Write up your findings with quotes from the person you interviewed.

4. Go to the library and find a popular magazine for the years covered by your interview. Write a two page comparison of how what you read compares with what the interview revealed.

Name _____

Exercise 12.3

Use the computer CD that comes with the workbook for this exercise and connect to the Internet. Follow the instructions in the workbook preface. From the table of contents, go to Chapter 14 - Comparative.

Go to the web site called International Statistics from OECD,

1. At the web click on to **Statistics** (left side near top under FIND).
2. On the left side under "Data by Topic" select Education and Skills. Click on it. Locate one of the tables and print it.
3. Locate the "Statistics Brief" on the far right side bar toward the bottom).
4. Write a one-age essay in which you discuss the tables/charts you printed from steps 2 and 3.

Exercise 12.4

Go Chapter 12 in the Student Workbook and lick on the list of Oral History Projects (Michigan State University) http://www.h-net.msu.edu/~oralhist/projects.html.

Pick a topic and read the oral history materials (or listen to tapes/watch videos). Write a one page essay one what you learned about the historical period based upon the short narrations you read from the two oral histories. Give the names of the people who were the narrators.

CHAPTER 13

ANALYZING QUALITATIVE DATA

LEARNING OBJECTIVES

After studying Chapter 13 you will be able to do the following:
1. Describe how quantitative and qualitative data analysis differ from each other;
2. Discuss purpose of the three types of qualitative data coding and the use of analytic memos;
3. Describe at several different ways to conduct qualitative data analysis;

KEY TERMS MATCHING DEFINITIONS, CHAPTER 13

1. A first coding of qualitative data in which a researcher examines the data to condense them into preliminary analytic categories or codes for analyzing the data.
2. A second coding of qualitative data after open coding. The researcher organizes the codes, develops links among them, and discovers key analytic categories.
3. A last pass at coding qualitative data in which a researcher examines previous codes to identify and select illustrative data that will support the conceptual coding categories that he or she developed.
4. A name for conceptual categories in an explanation that a researcher uses as part of the illustrative method of qualitative data analysis.
5. A method of qualitative data analysis in which a researcher takes the concepts of a social theory or explanation and treats them as empty boxes to be filled with empirical examples and descriptions.
6. A method of qualitative data analysis in which the researcher repeatedly moves back and forth between the empirical data and the abstract concepts, theories or models.
7. A type of historical or field research writing that is also a form of qualitative data analysis. The analysis consists of "telling a story" that presents information chronologically, following specific people or events.

Name _____

MATCHING KEY TERMS FOR CHAPTER 13

	Axial coding		Open coding
	Empty boxes		Selective Coding
	Illustrative method		Successive approximation
	Narrative history		

Exercise 13.1

Locate a scholarly article based on qualitative data. Here are some good journals to look at. Be careful. The study should be field research/ethnography or historical-comparative.
- *Comparative Studies in Society and History*
- *Ethnography*
- *Field Research*
- *International Journal of Comparative Sociology*
- *Journal of Contemporary Ethnography*
- *Journal of Historical Sociology*
- *Qualitative Inquiry*
- *Social Problems*
- *Social Science History*

Provide a photocopy of the article. After reading the article answer the following:

1. Did the author use any of the types of qualitative data analysis described in chapter 15 as part of the article? If so which one?
2. Think of an example of a type of event or data which did NOT appear or which did not occur. What did not occur? How would finding such "negative evidence" affect the conclusions of the article?

Exercise 13.2

Develop a flowchart of a social activity that you have participated in or will soon participate in (e.g., getting a driver's license, organizing a wedding). See the example of cake making in the textbook.

In your example include **at least 20 parts** or steps in the process and label them clearly.

Name _____

PRACTICE QUIZ 6, Chapters 11-13 (12 questions)

1. When analyzing her qualitative data, Kathy King made a pass through her notes skimming her previous codes and notes. She looked for major themes that organized the codes. This is called:

   a. Open coding
   b. Axial coding
   c. Selective coding
   d. Contingency coding
   e. Divergent coding

2. Succi Storm developed an abstract model of the "perfect" rock music group. Her model included six factors: clear beat in the music, high-level of on stage performance excitement, new electronic sound, dramatic dress and appearance of the performers, distinctiveness of the sound, and degree to which lyrics are relevant to young people's problems. She evaluated 20 groups that were performing on the New York City night club circuit by seeing how well each fit her model. In terms of qualitative data analysis, she had created a(n):

   a. Oral history
   b. Selective approximation
   c. Axial code
   d. Ideal type

3. The general name for a style of writing history in which the author tells a story and provides many details about the specific events and people, usually in chronological order, is:

   a. Recollections
   b. Running records
   c. Analytic memo
   d. Oral history
   e. Narrative history

4. What would you find in the **Human Relations Area Files**?

   a. Organized records of field research studies on many small, isolated pre-industrial societies or tribal groups.
   b. Statistical records that provide quantitative information on many different countries.
   c. Data on individual as unit of analysis that mixes qualitative and quantitative information.
   d. Many oral history and life story records on people who live in five nations: Australia, the United States, Canada, Ireland, and Great Britain.
   e. Survey data on early survey research, those conducted before 1950.

5. Andrew Hiroshi is conducting a study in which he is examining the diaries and letters of immigrants written 50 years ago. He was especially concerned about what the immigration said about their new society. He wants what immigrants actually said, not something they were repeating from what others told them. Andrew looks for consistency within the written documents. He also considers how the diaries and letters reflect the context in which they were written. He is concerned with:

   a. external criticism
   b. internal criticism
   c. courtesy bias
   d. Galton's problem

6. When listening to the day care worker, Mary, explain how her divorce proceedings were going, Sally became bored and began to daydream. Yet, she smiled, nodded her head, and put on a "front" of acting as if she really cared about what Mary said. Sally was using the technique of:

   a. Attitude of Strangeness
   b. Defocusing
   c. Appearance of Interest
   d. Normalize

7. Validity is achieved in field research in several ways. One way, the degree to which the social world described by a researcher matches the world of members under study in a way that would have occurred without the researcher being present, is called,

   a. Natural history
   b. Ecological Validity
   c. Member validation
   d. Competent insider performance
   e. None of the above

8. The field researcher should **NOT** do which of the following when coding field notes and beginning the analysis of data?

   a. Draw pictures or models to help organize thoughts.
   b. Try to describe what is happening or explain his/her findings by substituting different words until reaching one that feels right.
   c. Keep one set of categories from the first day in the field until finished writing the final report.
   d. File in chronological order the field notes taken each day quickly, and don't let them pile up in an unorganized mess.
   e. Constantly compare situations or items under analysis to stimulate thinking about the field setting and events.

9. Going native in field research refers to:

   a. Overinvolvement or overparticipation by the researcher.
   b. Taking notes while in the field.
   c. The first day in the field.
   d. Using the subjects' terms for events
   e. Doing field research on rural, primitive people.

10. When conducting a field research interview, the researcher should:

    a. write out all the questions to be asked in advance, and ask each question in order exactly as worded to prevent bias.
    b. not let person being interviewed ever interrupt the interview, interject anything or switch the topic.
    c. not reveal his or her person views in the interview and never add any extra words during the interview that may influence the person being interviewed.
    d. engage in a dialogue, the researcher and person in the field ask and answer questions of one another to share feelings, impressions and ideas.
    e. a and d

11. Which of the following is FALSE about field research?

    a. Researchers usually use an inductive method of inquiry.
    b. Researchers often use grounded theory.
    c. Researchers test precisely planned hypotheses.
    d. A researcher spends a lot of time in a field setting in direct contact the people he or she is studying.
    e. Researchers often begin a study with only vague, loose ideas about what they will discover.

12. Of types of field notes mentioned in the book, which one will take the largest amount of space or paper to write up?

    a. Direct Observation (usually in chronological order)
    b. Inferences
    c. Jotted Noted
    d. Analytic Memos
    e. Personal Journal

Chapter 14

WRITING THE RESEARCH REPORT

LEARNING OBJECTIVES

After studying Chapter 14 you will be able to do the following:
1. Understand the basic steps of the writing process as it applies to social science research reports.
2. Discuss strategies for organizing the writing tasks and the content of a research report.
3. Explain differences in the basic structure of quantitative and qualitative research reports.
4. Understand the process of grant-writing or "grantsmanship" and requests for proposals.

KEY TERMS MATCHING DEFINITIONS, CHAPTER 14

1. A summary of a research project's findings placed at the beginning of report for an applied, non-specialist audience, usually a little longer than an abstract.
2. A mistake that can occur when writing qualitative research in which a writer separates concrete empirical details from abstract ideas too much.
3. A method of organizing a field research report in which the author begins broadly with a topic, then increasingly focuses it more narrowly and specifically
4. A step in the writing process that is part of rewriting in which a writer adds ideas or evidence, and deletes, rearranges or changes ideas to improve clarity and better communicate meaning.
5. When a writer uses the words and the ideas of another person, but fails to document properly the original source.
6. An early step in the writing process during which a writer organizes notes, makes lists of ideas, outlines thoughts and makes certain that bibliographic citations are complete.
7. The person who is primarily in charge of research on a project that is sponsored or funded by an organization.
8. Strategies and skills of locating appropriate funding sources and preparing quality proposals to fund research
9. An announcement by a funding organization that it is willing to fund research and it is soliciting written plans of research projects.
10. A step in the writing process in which the writer goes over a previous draft to improve communication of ideas and clarity of expression.
11. A step in the writing process in which a writer cleans up and tightens the language and checks grammar, verb agreement, usage, sentence length, and paragraph organization to improve communication.
12. When a writer restates or rewords the ideas of another person, giving proper credit to the original source.

Name _____

MATCHING KEY TERMS FOR CHAPTER 14

	editing		prewriting
	error of segregation		principal investigator (PI)
	executive summary		request for proposals (RFP)
	grantsmanship		revising
	paraphrasing		rewriting
	plagiarism		zoom lens

Name _____

Exercise 14.1

Determine whether your college or university has an office devoted to research grants (sometimes called sponsored research or extramural research). Visit the office and ask how you could find two **Request For Proposals** for a topic for a professor/teacher that you know. Get all the documentation for the RFP's including length, outline, etc. that may be required. Ideally, get RFP's issued by two different funding organizations or agencies so you can compare them. If the office has a copy of a full grant proposal that has been submitted, whether or not it has been funded, ask if you can borrow it. From the two RFP's and the grant proposal, answer the following questions:

- What evidence, if any, is there that the author should be familiar with the scholarly literature on a topic.

- How detailed is the description of the process of doing the research that is being proposed?

- How important does the background of the person going to do the research appear to be.

- Does budget part of the proposals seem to be very relevant?

Name _____

PRACTICE QUIZ 7, CHAPTER 14 (4 questions)

1. What is using another's ideas, but rewording or restating them in one's own words, boiling down the ideas to their essence and giving credit to the original source.

    a. Prewriting
    b. Paraphrasing
    c. Plagiarism
    d. Editing
    e. Revising

2. In the writing process, in which step should you devote efforts to grammar, spelling, proper word choice, and sentence structure, and so forth?

    a. Prewriting
    b. Editing
    c. Rewriting
    d. Revising
    e. Freewriting

3. Which of the following is often found in a qualitative field research report, but rarely in a research report based on quantitative data from a survey or experiment?

    a. A separate section labeled Methods or Data
    b. A hypothesis or problem definition section
    c. A section of results that presents, but does not discuss or interpret data, followed by a discussion section.
    d. A "natural history" style of organization
    e. A tight, highly condensed style of presentation that often avoids first person (i.e., I next did this).

4. Advice for the style for writing a good research report includes:

    a. Use very specialized technical sociological terms everywhere you can so that the professor and other readers will be impressed that know that you are an informed person.
    b. Include as many thoughts or ideas in each sentence as possible to save space and "pack in" the information.
    c. Use active rather than passive voice verbs, example of passive voice verb is "door opened" and active verb is "he opened the door."
    d. Use flowery, colorful adverbs and adjectives and the biggest words you can find whenever possible to make the paper sound intelligent.

APPENDIX A
ANSWERS TO PRACTICE QUIZZES AND MATCHING

PRACTICE QUIZ 1 (Chapters 1-2)

1. B 2. A 3. E 4. C 5. D 6. D 7. B 8. B 9. B 10. E

PRACTICE QUIZ 2 (Chapters 3-4)

1. D 2. B 3. E 4. E 5. D 6. D 7. A 8. C 9. C 10. C

11. A 12. D 13. B 14. B 15. B 16. A 17. E 18. B

PRACTICE QUIZ 3 (Chapters 5-6)

1. D 2. D 3. C 4. C 5. B 6. A 7. E 8. E 9. C 10. E

11. B 12. D 13. C 14. B 15. E 16. C

PRACTICE QUIZ 4 (Chapters 7-8)

1. D 2. E 3. C 4. A 5. E 6. B 7. D 8. D 9. C 10. D

11. C 12. C 13. A 14. D 15. B 16. A 17. A 18. E

PRACTICE QUIZ 5 (Chapters 9-10)

1. A 2. D 3. E 4. C 5. C 6. C 7. A 8. D 9. E 10. D

11. B 12. E

PRACTICE QUIZ 6 (Chapters 11-13)

1. B 2. D 3. E 4. A 5. B 6. C 7. B 8. C 9. A 10. D

11. C 12. A

PRACTICE QUIZ 7 (Chapter 14)

1. B 2. B 3. D 4. C

ANSWER KEY TO MATCHING QUESTIONS

CHAPTER 1: DOING SOCIAL RESEARCH

25	Action-Oriented Research	9	Halo Effect
16	Applied Research	17	Historical-Comparative Research
18	Basic Research	29	Longitudinal Research
11	Case-Study Research	6	Overgeneralization
24	Cohort Analysis	14	Panel Study
15	Cross-Sectional Research	7	Premature Closure
3	Data	30	Qualitative Data
22	Descriptive Research	5	Quantitative Data
1	Empirical Evidence	4	Selective Observation
13	Evaluation Research	2	Scientific Community
23	Existing Statistics Research	8	Scientific Method
19	Experimental Research	25	Social Impact Assessment
20	Explanatory Research	10	Social Research
28	Exploratory Research	21	Survey Research
12	Field Research	27	Time Series Research

CHAPTER 2: THEORY AND SOCIAL RESEARCH

3	Association	23	Macro-Level
11	Assumption	22	Meso-Level
25	Blame Analysis	7	Micro-Level
4	Causal Explanation	14	Negative Relationship
1	Classification	17	Nomothetic
2	Concept Cluster	20	Paradigm
13	Deductive Approach	24	Positive Relationship
8	Empirical Generalization	19	Praxis
15	Functional Theory	5	Prediction
12	Grounded Theory	9	Proposition
6	Ideal Type	21	Replication
18	Idiographic	16	Verstehen
11	Inductive Approach		

CHAPTER 3: ETHICS IN SOCIAL RESEARCH

5	Anonymity	9	Principle of Voluntary Consent
4	Confidentiality	12	Public Sociology
10	Cross-over Design	2	Research Fraud
1	Informed Consent	8	Scientific Misconduct
6	Institutional Review Board (IRB)	11	Special Population
3	Plagiarism	7	Whistleblower

CHAPTER 4: REVIEWING THE SCHOLARLY LITERATURE AND PLANNING A STUDY

14	Abstract	18	Linear Research Path
16	Alternate Hypothesis	23	Literature Review
2	Attributes	12	Logic of Disconfirming Hypotheses
15	Citation	19	Non-Linear Research Path
9	Dependent Variable	8	Null Hypothesis
10	Ecological Fallacy	11	Reductionism
20	First Order Interpretation	21	Second Order Interpretation
13	Hypothesis	6	Spuriousness
3	Independent Variable	22	Third-Order Interpretation
4	Intervening Variable	1	Unit of Analysis
7	Level of Analysis	3	Universe
		17	Variable

CHAPTER 5: QUALITATIVE & QUANTITATIVE MEASUREMENT

33	Bogardus Social Distance Scale	10	Levels of Measurement
22	Conceptual Definition	28	Likert Scale
7	Conceptual Hypothesis	1	Measurement Validity
5	Conceptualization	26	Multiple Indicators
14	Concurrent Validity	30	Mutually Exclusive Attributes
16	Content Validity	11	Nominal-Level Measurement
22	Continuous Variables	17	Operational Definition
13	Criterion Validity	6	Operationalization
23	Discrete Variables	18	Ordinal-Level Measurement
8	Empirical Hypothesis	15	Predictive Validity
31	Exhaustive Attributes	12	Ratio-Level Measurement
25	External Validity	2	Reliability
4	Face Validity	34	Scale
33	Guttman Scale	29	Semantic Differential
28	Index	3	Standardization
24	Internal Validity	9	Unidimensionality
19	Interval-Level Measurement	20	Validity

CHAPTER 6: QUALITATIVE & QUANITATIVE SAMPLING

21	Central Limit Theorem	26	Sample
18	Cluster Sampling	20	Sampling Distribution
22	Confidence Intervals	7	Sampling Element
27	Deviant Case Sampling	17	Sampling Error
15	Haphazard Sampling	10	Sampling Frame
28	Hidden Populations	12	Sampling Interval
24	Inferential Statistics	11	Sampling Ratio
29	Nonrandom Sample	31	Sequential Sampling
3	Parameter	1	Simple Random Sampling
8	Population	4	Snowball Sampling
19	Probability Proportionate to Size [PPS]	2	Sociogram
14	Purposive Sampling	25	Statistic
5	Quota Sampling	6	Stratified Sampling
13	Random Digit Dialing [RDD]	23	Systematic Sampling
16	Random Number Table	9	Target Population
30	Random Sample		

CHAPTER 7: SURVEY RESEARCH

5	Closed-Ended Question	6	Open-ended Question
20	Computer Assisted Telephone Interviewing CATI	13	Order Effects
14	Context Effects	7	Partially-Open Question
21	Contingency Question	1	Prestige Bias
16	Cover sheet	4	Probe
3	Double-barreled Question	18	Quasi-Filter Question
10	Floaters	12	Response Set
19	Full-Filter Question	8	Social Desirability Bias
15	Funnel Sequence	22	Standard-Format Question
2	Interview Schedule	9	Threatening Questions
17	Matrix Question	11	Wording Effects

CHAPTER 8: EXPERIMENTAL RESEARCH

32	Control Group	13	Latin Square Design
18	Classical Experimental Design	17	Maturation
5	Debrief	7	Mortality
11	Deception	19	One Shot Case Study
21	Design Notation	1	Placebo
12	Diffusion of Treatment	15	Posttest
23	Double Blind Experiment	30	Pre-experimental Designs
27	Equivalent Time Series	14	Pretest
8	Experimental Design	31	Quasi-Experimental Designs
26	Experimental Group	9	Random Assignment
6	Factorial Design	29	Reactivity
24	Field Experiment	3	Selection Bias
16	Hawthorne Effect	22	Solomon Four Group Design
20	History Effects	28	Static Group Comparison
33	Interaction Effects	2	Subjects
10	Interrupted Time Series Design	4	Treatment
25	Laboratory Experiment		

CHAPTER 9: NONREACTIVE & SECONDARY ANALYSIS

2	Accretion Measures	7	Manifest Coding
5	Coding	11	Nonreactive
4	Coding System	12	Recording Sheet
15	Content analysis	9	*Statistical Abstract of the U.S.*
3	Erosion measures	13	Structured Observation
14	Fallacy of misplaced concreteness	6	Text
10	General Social Survey (GSS)	1	Unobtrusive measures
8	Latent coding		

CHAPTER 10: ANALYSIS OF QUANTITATIVE DATA

29	Bar chart	30	Marginals
35	Bivariate statistics	5	Mean
12	Body of a table	4	Median
13	Cell of a table	3	Mode
9	Code sheets	40	Normal distribution
1	Codebook	28	Partials
23	Contingency cleaning	7	Percentile
2	Contingency table	10	Pie chart
15	Control variable	24	Possible code cleaning
36	Covariation	6	Range
11	Cross-tabulation	18	Replication pattern
38	Curvilinear relationship	25	Scattergram
39	Descriptive statistics	32	Skewed distribution
16	Direct entry method	22	Specification pattern
17	Elaboration paradigm	8	Standard deviation
20	Explanation pattern	43	Statistical significance
33	Frequency distribution	21	Suppressor variable pattern
34	Frequency polygon	41	Type I error
26	Independence	42	Type II error
19	Interpretation pattern	27	Univariate statistics
31	Level of statistical significance	14	Z score
37	Linear relationship		

CHAPTER 11: FIELD RESEARCH

9	Analytic Memos	10	Field site
4	Appearance of interest	20	Focus group
6	Attitude of Strangeness	1	Go native
14	Contrast question	18	Guilty Knowledge
12	Descriptive question	21	Internal Consistency
7	Direct Observation Notes	8	Jotted notes
19	Ecological validity	15	Member validation
2	Ethnographic Fallacy	3	Naturalism
17	Ethnography	5	Normalize social research
16	Ethnomethodology	13	Structural question
11	External Consistency		

CHAPTER 12: HISTORICAL-COMPARATIVE RESEARCH

1	Back translation	7	Lexicon equivalence
6	Conceptual Equivalence	8	Measurement equivalence
5	Contextual Equivalence	14	Oral history
3	External criticism	9	Primary sources
10	Galton's Problem	12	Recollections
4	Human Relations Area Files (HRAF)	13	Running records
2	Internal Criticism	11	Secondary Sources

CHAPTER 13: ANALYSIS OF QUALITATIVE DATA			
2	Axial coding	2	Open coding
4	Empty boxes	3	Selective Coding
5	Illustrative method	6	Successive approximation
7	Narrative		

CHAPTER 14: WRITING A RESEARCH REPORT			
11	Editing	6	Prewriting
2	Error of segregation	7	Principal investigator (PI)
1	Executive summary	9	Request for proposals (RFP)
8	Grantsmanship	4	Revising
12	Paraphrasing	10	Rewriting
5	Plagiarism	3	Zoom Lens

Summary of Number of Key Terms and Exercises by Chapter

Chapter	Number of Key Terms	Number of Exercises
1	30	5
2	25	3
3	12	4
4	22	5
5	34	7
6	31	4
7	22	5
8	33	5
9	15	5
10	43	4
11	21	3
12	14	3
13	7	2
14	12	1
Total	321	56

APPENDIX B
CONTENTS OF DATA FILES

DATA FILE: Gender Issues
Extracted from 2004 General Social Survey.
47 Variables, 1331 cases (number of cases varies by variable)
(3 copies in SPSS portable, Excel and Microcase formats)

VARIABLE	QUESTION IN GENERAL SOCIAL SURVEY
1 MARITAL	Are you currently married, widowed, divorced, separated, or have you never been married?
2 DIVORCE?	*Asked only of currently married or widowed*: Have you ever been divorced or legally separated?
3 MATEWORK	*Asked only of currently married* Last week was your (husband/wife) working full time, part time, going to school, keeping house, or what?
4 AGE	Respondent's Age
5 EDUCATION	What is the highest grade in elementary school or high school that you finished and got credit for?
6 SEX	Respondent's sex.
7 RACE	Respondent's race.
8 INCOME	In which group was your total family income, from all sources, last year before taxes, that is?
9 REGION	Region of the United States where interview took place.
10 RELIGION	What is your religious preference? Is it Protestant, Catholic, Jewish, some other religion, or no religion?
11 WATCHTV	On an average day, how many hours do you personally watch television?
12 DEGREE	Highest education degree earned by Respondent.
13 PRAY	About how often do you pray?
14 AFFMACT	Do you favor or oppose preference in hiring and promotion, strongly or not strongly?
15 POL. PARTY	Generally speaking, do you think of yourself as a Republican, Democrat, Independent, or what?
16 PRES 2000	If voted in 2000 election, did you vote for Al Gore or George W. Bush?
17 POL. VIEW	Using a 7-point scale on which the political views that people might hold from extremely liberal to extremely conservative, where would you place yourself?
18 MAN DISCR	What are the chances these days that a man won't get a job or promotion while an equally or less qualified woman will? Is this very likely, somewhat likely, not likely, or not very likely?
19 FEM JOB	Some people say because of past discrimination a woman should be given a preference in hiring and promotion. Others say that preferences in hiring and promotion of women is wrong because it discriminates again men. What is your opinion? Are you for or against a hiring and promotion preference for women?
20 WMN DISCR	What are the chances these days that a woman won't get a job or promotion while an equally or less qualified man will? Is this very likely, somewhat likely, not likely, or not very likely?
21 HIRE WOMEN	How much do you agree/disagree with the following statement: Because of past discrimination employers should make special efforts to hire and promote qualified women.
22 # CHILDREN	How many children have you ever had? Please count all that were born alive and include ones you had from a past marriage.
23 AGE KD BRN	How old were you when your first child was born?
24 DAD DEGRE	Highest educational degree of respondent's father
25 MOM DEGREE	Highest educational degree of respondent's mother

26	MATE DEGREE	Highest educational degree of respondent's spouse
27	FAMILY @ 16	Were you living with both your mother and father around the age of 16? If no, who were you living with?
28	ATTEND	How often do you attend religious services?
29	SCHL PRAY	The United States Supreme Court has ruled that no state or local government may require the reading of the Lord's Prayer in public schools. What is your opinion? Do you agree or disagree with this court ruling?
30	SEX ED?	Would you be for or against sex education in the public schools?
31	SEX FREQ	About how often did you have sex during the past 12 months?
32	XMAR SEX	What is your opinion about married peson having sex with someone other than the marriage partner?
33	PREM SEX	There's been a lot of discussion about the way morals and attitudes about sex are changing in this country. If a man and woman have sex relations before marriage, do you think it is always wrong, almost always wrong, wrong only sometimes, or not wrong at all?
34	HAP.MARR	*IF CURRENTLY MARRIED*: Taking things all together, how would you describe your marriage? Would you say that your marriage is very happy, pretty happy, or not too happy?
35	SPANKING	Do you strongly agree, agree, disagree, or strongly disagree that it is sometimes necessary to discipline a child with a good, hard spanking?
36	EUTHANAS	When a person has an incurable disease, should doctors be allowed by law to end the patient's life by a painless means if the patient and his family request it?
37	NEWSPAPER	How often do you read the newspaper—every day, a few times a week, once a week, less than once a week, or never?
38	WIFE@HOME	It is much better for everyone involved if the man is the achiever outside the home and the woman takes care of the home and family.
39	MEN BETTER	Do you agree or disagree with this statement: Most men are better suited emotionally for politics than are most women.
40	PRESCH.WRK	Agree/Disagree A preschool child is likely to suffer if his or her mother works..
41	ABORT DEFECT	LEGAL ABORTION OK: If the fetus has a serious defect?
42	ABORT WANT	LEGAL ABORTION OK: If a woman does not want a child?
43	ABORT HEALTH	LEGAL ABORTION OK: If there are serious health risks for the woman?
44	ABORT POOR	LEGAL ABORTION OK: If the woman cannot afford to raise a child?
45	ABORT RAPE	LEGAL ABORTION OK: If the woman became pregnant as the result of rape?
46	ABORT SINGLE	LEGAL ABORTION OK: If the woman is unmarried?
47	ABORT ANY	LEGAL ABORTION OK: For any reason a woman wants?

DATA FILE: Race-Ethnicity Issues.
Extracted from 2004 General Social Survey
44 Variables, 1276 cases (number of cases varies by variable)
(3 copies in SPSS portable, Excel and Microcase formats)

VARIABLE	QUESTION IN GENERAL SOCIAL SURVEY
1 MARITAL	Are you currently married, widowed, divorced, separated, or have you never been married?
2 DIVORCE?	*Asked only of currently married or widowed*: Have you ever been divorced or legally separated?
3 MATEWORK	*Asked only of currently married*: Last week was your (husband/wife) working full time, part time, going to school, keeping house, or what?
4 AGE	Respondent's Age
5 EDUCATION	What is the highest grade in elementary school or high school that you finished and got credit for?
6 SEX	Respondent's sex.
7 RACE	Respondent's race.
8 INCOME	In which group was your total family income, from all sources, last year before taxes, that is?
9 REGION	Region of the United States where interview took place.
10 RELIGION	What is your religious preference? Is it Protestant, Catholic, Jewish, some other religion, or no religion?
11 WATCHTV	On an average day, how many hours do you personally watch television?
12 GOVBLACK	What do you think about the government helping Blacks, using a 1–5 scale where 1 = Strongly Agree the government is obligated to help Blacks, to 5 = Strongly Agree that the government shouldn't give special treatment.
13 SELF EMP	(Are/Were) you self employed or (do/did) you work for someone else?
14 DADSLFEMP	While you were going up was your father self employed or did he work for someone else?
15 DEGREE	Highest education degree earned by Respondent.
16 URBAN@ 16	Which category on this card comes closest to the type of place you were living in when 16? Farm/Country, Under 50,000, 50,000–250,000 people, suburb, over 250,000 people
17 BORNUSA	Were you born in this country?
18 POL. PARTY	Generally speaking, do you think of yourself as a Republican, Democrat, Independent, or what?
19 PRES 2000	If voted in 2000 election, did you vote for Al Gore or George W. Bush?
20 POL. VIEW	Using a 7-point scale on which the political views that people might hold from extremely liberal to extremely conservative, where would you place yourself?
21 SPENDBLK	Government spending on improving the conditions of Blacks is:
22 EXECUTE?	Do you favor or oppose the death penalty for persons convicted of murder?
23 GUN LAW?	Would you favor or oppose a law which would require a person to obtain a police permit before he or she could buy a gun?
24 PRAY	About how often do you pray?
25 AFFMACT	Do you favor or oppose preference in hiring and promotion, strongly or not strongly?
26 PISTOL?	*IF YES TO OWNGUN?:* Is it a pistol?
27 RACEDIF1	On average Blacks have worse jobs, income and housing than Whites, is this mainly due to discrimination?
28 RACEDIF2	On average Blacks have worse jobs, income and housing than Whites, is this because most Blacks have less in-born ability to learn?
29 RACEDIF4	On average Blacks have worse jobs, income and housing than Whites, is this because most Blacks don't have the motivation or will power to pull themselves out of poverty?

30 MARRYBLK — *Not asked of Blacks.* How would you respond to a close relative marrying a Black person?

31 BLACK WORK — On a 1–7 scale, where 1 is hard working and 7 is lazy, where would you place Blacks?

32 REVDISCR — What do you think the chances are these days that a White person won't get a job or promotion, while an equally or less qualified Black person gets one instead?

33 MELTNGPOT — Some people say it is better for American if different racial or ethnic groups maintain their distinct culture. Others argue that it is better if they blend into the larger society as in the idea of a melting pot. Where do you place yourself on the following scale: From 1, different racial and ethnic groups should maintain their distinct cultures, to 7 groups should blend into the larger society.

34 LET IN — Do you think the number of immigration from foreign countries who are permitted to come to the United States to live should be increased or decreased?

35 IMM. CRIME — Do you agree or disagree with this statement: Immigrants cause crime?

36 IMM ECON — Do you agree or disagree with this statement: Immigrants are generally good for America's economy?

37 IMM JOBS — Do you agree or disagree with this statement: Immigrants take jobs from people who were born in America?

38 IMM RIGHTS — Legal immigrants who are not citizens should have the same rights as American citizens.

39 RACIST INDEX — Sum of these six variables MARRY BLACK+ WORK BLACK + GOV BLACK + RACE DIF 1 + RACE DIF 2 + RACE DIF 4.
Each was first recoded as 0 or 1, with 1 indicating a more racist view.

40 BLACK IQ — How would you rate the intelligence of Blacks on 1–7 scale, 1 = unintelligent and 7 = intelligent.

41 LIVE BLACK — Would you favor living in a neighborhood where one-half of your neighbors were Black?

42 WORK UP — Do you Agree or Disagree with the statement: Irish, Italians, Jewish and many other minorities overcame prejudice and worked their way up. Blacks should do the same without special favors.

43 CLOSE BLACK — How close do you feel toward Blacks, where 1 is not close and 9 is very close.

44 FAIR HOUSE — Select one of the following:
(a) A law says a homeowner can decide for himself whom to sell his house to, even if he prefers not to sell to Blacks/ African Americans,
(b) A second law says a homeowner cannot refuse to sell his house because of their race or color.

NOTES

NOTES

NOTES

NOTES

NOTES

NOTES

NOTES